THE ART OF WOODWORKING

KITCHEN CABINETS

THE ART OF WOODWORKING

KITCHEN CABINETS

TIME-LIFE BOOKS
ALEXANDRIA, VIRGINIA

ST. REMY PRESS
MONTREAL

THE ART OF WOODWORKING was produced by
ST. REMY PRESS

PUBLISHER	Kenneth Winchester
PRESIDENT	Pierre Léveillé
Series Editor	Pierre Home-Douglas
Series Art Director	Francine Lemieux
Editor	Andrew Jones
Art Directors	Jean-Pierre Bourgeois, Normand Boudreau
Designers	François Daxhelet, Jean-Guy Doiron
Picture Editor	Geneviève Monette
Writers	John Dowling, Adam Van Sertima
Contributing Illustrators	Gilles Beauchemin, Michel Blais, Ronald Durepos, Jacques Perrault, Michael Stockdale, James Thérien
Administrator	Natalie Watanabe
Production Manager	Michelle Turbide
Coordinator	Dominique Gagné
System Coordinator	Eric Beaulieu
Photographer	Robert Chartier
Proofreader	Judy Yelon
Indexer	Christine M. Jacobs

Time-Life Books is a division of Time Life Inc.,
a wholly owned subsidiary of
THE TIME INC. BOOK COMPANY

TIME-LIFE INC.

President and CEO	John M. Fahey

TIME-LIFE BOOKS

President	John D. Hall
Managing Editor	Roberta Conlan
Director of Design	Michael Hentges
Director of Editorial Operations	Ellen Robling
Consulting Editor	John R. Sullivan
Vice-President, Book Production	Marjann Caldwell
Production Manager	Marlene Zack
Quality Assurance Manager	James King

THE CONSULTANTS

Jon Eakes has been a cabinetmaker and custom renovator in Montreal for more than 20 years. He is known primarily for his teaching through books, videos, radio, and the TV show *Renovation Zone.*

Giles Miller-Mead taught advanced cabinetmaking at Montreal technical schools for more than ten years. A native of New Zealand, he has worked as a restorer of antique furniture.

Kitchen cabinets.
       p. cm. — (The Art of woodworking)
    Includes index.
    ISBN 0-8094-9545-7
    1. Kitchen-cabinets. 2. Cabinetwork.
    I. Time-Life Books. II. Series.
    TT197.5.K57 1996
    684.1'6—dc20   95-46501
                                                        CIP

For information about any Time-Life book,
please call 1-800-621-7026, or write:
Reader Information
Time-Life Customer Service
P.O. Box C-32068
Richmond, Virginia
23261-2068

CONTENTS

Tom Santarsiero on
CHOOSING CABINET STYLES

Despite the tremendous variety of kitchen cabinets, they all come down to two basic types: face frame and frameless. Each has characteristics that greatly affect how the heart of the modern home will appear and function. For the designer, cabinetmaker, and installer, they also determine how the cabinets will be created.

Face frame cabinets are the most popular type of kitchen cabinet in North America. This time-honored method of construction involves attaching a framework of solid lumber to the front of a carcase. Doors and drawers can be mounted in one of three ways: inset, lipped, or overlay. Inset, the most elegant in appearance, is a true test of a craftsman's skill in construction and installation. Tight tolerances are required to accommodate seasonal wood movement and yield a pleasing margin between frame and door. During installation, cabinets must be set perfectly level and plumb to maintain that margin. My clients who choose framed cabinets are very interested in forging a link with the past. They appreciate the classic look of well-fitted doors and drawers that open with ease and close with a gentle puff of air as they nest within the frame.

Frameless cabinetry was born in Europe after World War II. It addressed some of the challenges of the time, such as the shortage of lumber and the need to rebuild housing rapidly. The simplicity of the frameless, or European, kitchen cabinet greatly reduced material, needs, and production time. Doors would align tightly together, creating a clean, flowing line of casework. This reflected a modernist view of a changed world where time was short and production and efficiency reigned supreme. This construction method yielded other benefits. Drawers could be wider and deeper because they didn't need to clear a face frame. And storage and removal of items along with cleaning the cabinet interior became easier and more efficient.

Today, the line between face frame and frameless casework has blurred slightly. Frameless cabinets are no longer limited to flush-laminate doors; most of the frameless kitchens I build feature traditional raised panel doors, multi-part cornice moldings, and other accoutrements endowing each kitchen with warmth and comfort. For building, installing, maximizing storage, and ease of use, frameless cabinets can't be surpassed. If, on the other hand, you'd prefer a touch of timeless tradition in your kitchen, your cabinets are only a face frame away.

Tom Santarsiero is President of the Kitchen Design Center in Montclair, New Jersey.

Donald Silvers discusses
KITCHEN FORM AND FUNCTION

In my work as a kitchen designer, I am continually juggling two requirements: creating spaces that are both wonderful to look at and a pleasure to work in. Form and function must work in tandem.

This was not always the case. In years past, cabinetmakers who designed kitchens were virtually unknown, since the homebuilder was responsible for creating the kitchen and its cabinets, and often brought to the kitchen the same economy of means with which he built the rest of the house. For example, a ceiling height of 8 feet and three studs spaced 16 inches apart created the need for large quantities of plywood. The homebuilder felt it was economically sound to use leftover plywood for kitchen cabinets so there would be no waste. The base cabinets were 22 inches deep and the wall cabinets were 11 to 12 inches deep. These cabinets—really just running shelves with doors—stubbornly resisted any form of change; base cabinets didn't change to a 24-inch depth until the development of dishwashers made it necessary.

In the kitchen environment of today, designing and building kitchens is much more than a way of recycling leftover homebuilding materials. To create eye-catching residential kitchens, today's designers have taken a cue from the extraordinary work of cabinetmakers. The different woods and finishes that make up the cabinetmaker's palette provide the freedom to conjure up any style. With his tools, the cabinetmaker might carve cherry or oak woods, creating French or English Country cabinets, or shape an intimate Arts and Crafts kitchen in beech. He could fashion an Art Deco look in the richness of walnut, or an Art Nouveau, Victorian, or Early American look in a variety of woods—pine, ash, maple, or mahogany, to name a few. The cabinetmaker might even work with laminates, putting at his disposal the entire color spectrum. And let's not forget the stains that produce an array of hues and patinas. The range of choices is breathtaking.

The cabinetmaker has also made the cook's life a delight by incorporating the right kind of accessories that can make the cook's job easier, even fun. For example, there are drawers and roll-outs with hardware that gives the cook fingertip control, pantries that are only a foot wide yet 84 inches tall, providing enormous storage when pulled out of a wall cabinet with ease. More and more, the kitchen designer of today is drawing on the past and the present to create a kitchen environment that looks and cooks beautifully.

Donald Silvers is a kitchen designer who teaches at the University of California at Los Angeles. He is the author of The Complete Guide To Kitchen Design With Cooking In Mind, *published by The Newark Management Institute.*

Sven Hanson talks about
A SMOOTH INSTALLATION

Kitchen cabinets need top-quality installation to look good and function well. Unlike fine furniture that can look good in a dusty corner of the shop, cabinets don't come to life until after they have been installed. Unfortunately, we tend to put off considering the problems of installation because it happens in an unfamiliar environment and requires skills different from those needed to build the cabinets.

To avoid these problems, start with and stick to a detailed installation plan, drawn up well before the cabinets are finished. Don't be tempted to change it because you suddenly like a 42-inch drop-in cooktop instead of the 36-inch one you originally planned for. This will force you to modify the range base, both adjacent cabinets, and their drawers. It's far more efficient to bring all parties to the negotiating table and make that kind of decision before you build the cabinets.

You will get to practice your psychological skills when you announce to the rest of the household that the kitchen will be closed for a few days while the new cabinets go in. Try to keep the blockade short and timed conveniently for everyone. Above all, do not fall into the snake pit of trying to have your new kitchen ready just before Thanksgiving or Christmas, investing in one of those "if everything goes to plan" schedules. However, if you plan to get rid of your in-laws while convincing them you are the complete idiot they thought, success beckons.

There is no right or wrong way to install cabinets. I like to install and level the plinths for the lower cabinets the afternoon before the installation begins. For sheer exhaustion, crawling around the floor to set all the bases level to the highest point of the floor stands apart from most woodworking chores. The following morning, I install the upper cabinets first, then the lower cabinets. As I screw the cabinets in place, I always double-check for levelness. Nothing says "idiot" louder than a tilting sink or cooktop. During installation, a dust curtain made of 4-mil plastic sheeting can repel would-be snackers while keeping most dust and some noise contained. To further reduce dust, you should block any air ducts and open the kitchen window a crack.

Finally, I've observed many first-time installers who use surprisingly few tools. I rely on many more and lay them out on a temporary workbench set at the edge of the room. If your shop is apart from the job site, start making a list of the installation tools while you're still constructing the cabinets. Visualizing the installation helps to fabricate a cabinet that is truly ready to install and helps organize your tools (and mindset) to finish the job properly. In 25 years I've never heard a single woodworker say, "I wish I hadn't wasted so much time preparing for that job."

Sven Hanson is a cabinetmaker
in Albuquerque, New Mexico.

LAYOUT AND DESIGN

The supply pipes and drain of a kitchen sink are marked on the wall with the aid of a carpenter's level (above). The precise location of the fixtures will then be marked onto vertical and horizontal site story poles before being transferred to the story poles for the sink cabinet itself.

S ince colonial days, the American kitchen has been thought of as the heart of the home. It is the first room a family shares each day; it is not only the place where meals are prepared, but also where they are often eaten. The kitchen is where children and adults do their homework, and where they linger for conversation. Yet, although the role of the kitchen has not changed in three centuries, its appearance has. Once, cooking was done by the central fireplace, and the larder was stored against the cold, north-facing wall. Today, a kitchen must be carefully planned to meet the demands of a busy household, and to accommodate a battery of labor-saving devices. This chapter focuses on the work of today's kitchen—especially its cabinetry—introduces popular designs, and outlines some basic principles that will help you create a kitchen that meets your needs.

A kitchen design often starts as a natural extension of the architectural style of a house. Just as trim, molding, and furnishings can distinguish a home as being Victorian or Colonial, cabinet doors, molding, and hardware can define the style of a kitchen. For example, Victorian is an opulent style marked by complex egg-and-dart molding, porcelain pulls, and exposed hinges, while Shaker style is a model of austerity, relying on simple, recessed frame-and-panel doors, an absence of molding, and the muted colors of milk paint. A gallery of kitchen styles from traditional to modern is shown starting on page 14.

Whether you choose a traditional architectural style for your kitchen or a blend of several styles, adequate room must be provided for work. The kitchen is a workshop like any other, and should be laid out with efficiency in mind. You would not think of locating the table saw and a planer at opposite ends of a workshop; the primary work centers of a kitchen—in most cases, the sink, refrigerator, and stove/cooking area—are no different. Work triangles *(page 17)* are one way to minimize the trips between the three.

Arriving at an efficient layout for a kitchen in a confined space can be a challenge. Invariably, the size and location of your kitchen cabinets will have to be flexible enough to accommodate the location of appliances, utilities, windows, and doors. A selection of basic layout options is shown on page 18. Drafting scale floor plans and elevations can help you visualize your layout; floor plans and elevations for a typical L-shaped kitchen are shown on page 20. Once you have settled on the placement of your cabinets, you can divide their runs into individual cabinets and drawers. While most kitchen cabinets adhere to basic dimensional standards in height *(page 19)*, their width and number of doors can be fine tuned to reach a visually well-balanced kitchen design *(page 22)*.

Accuracy is crucial when drafting floor plans and elevations. A site-referenced story pole *(page 24)* tells you everything you need to know about a kitchen wall in precise detail, including the location and size of the cabinets. By using these small lengths of wood for each wall and cabinet, you can proceed from floor plan to cutting list with a minimum of errors. From there to your dream kitchen it is only a few more careful steps.

Drawing your kitchen to scale is the best way to experiment with its layout. The photo at left shows the floor plan of an L-shaped kitchen, including the location of cabinets, windows, appliances, and utilities.

A GALLERY OF KITCHEN STYLES

While a kitchen should reflect your personal culinary needs and tastes, its design should not be chosen without first addressing a few important questions. Will the style complement or clash with the rest of the house architecturally? A Victorian kitchen would look out of place in a modern house decorated with Mission furniture. Budget is another important consideration. The lumber costs alone for an Arts and Crafts-style kitchen with cherry cabinets and frame-and-panel doors are beyond the reach of many. Popular, less expensive options include the European-style kitchen, which uses standardized melamine cabinets, or the Country-style kitchen, in which rustic

SHAKER

Many kitchens are Shaker-inspired, but few are as faithful to Shaker style as this house designed by architect Charles Allen Hill. With their flat recessed frame-and-panel doors, the cabinets eschew ornamentation, and evoke the Shaker's elegant yet utilitarian ethic. There's even a pegboard over the range.

VICTORIAN

Less opulent than its namesake, this kitchen designed by Maine architect John Gillespie nonetheless features several hallmarks of the style, most notably tall upper cabinets with tongue-and-groove doors, surface-mounted brass hinges, and porcelain pulls. Note the way the Victorian motifs—crown molding, ornate columns and arches —are carried into adjoining areas of the house.

charm can be derived from the minor defects of aged, recycled wood.

A kitchen design does not have to be faithful to a single style. As the gallery on these pages and the chart on page 16 show, several styles can be combined with a careful eye to create a unique design. Blending styles can make your design more flexible: Shaker-style kitchens are well-adapted to the modular construction of European-style cabinetry *(page 26)*. The discerning choice of the right materials can also unify a contrasting kitchen with the surrounding house. Cherry cabinets, for example, can provide a graceful transition between a European-style kitchen and a Colonial farmhouse.

EUROPEAN

Its hardware out of sight, the European-style cabinet defines the modern kitchen. Its clean, unadorned lines are enhanced by recessed lighting and plenty of uncluttered laminate countertop. Subtle touches by Maine designer John Scholtz, such as the porcelain frieze and backsplash trim and the ladderback Shaker chairs, lend a warm tone to the immaculate decor.

COLONIAL

This is an eclectic style that can be evoked as much by decoration as by actual cabinetry. Framed by exposed timbers, the kitchen at left, designed by Steven Foote of Boston, is a pleasingly modern update on the style. The brick, pine plank floors, and leaded glazing in the upper wall cabinets all contribute to a colonial ambiance. A more explicit reference to the style can be found in the frame-and-panel doors with oversized knobs.

DESIGN CHARACTERISTICS OF PERIOD STYLES

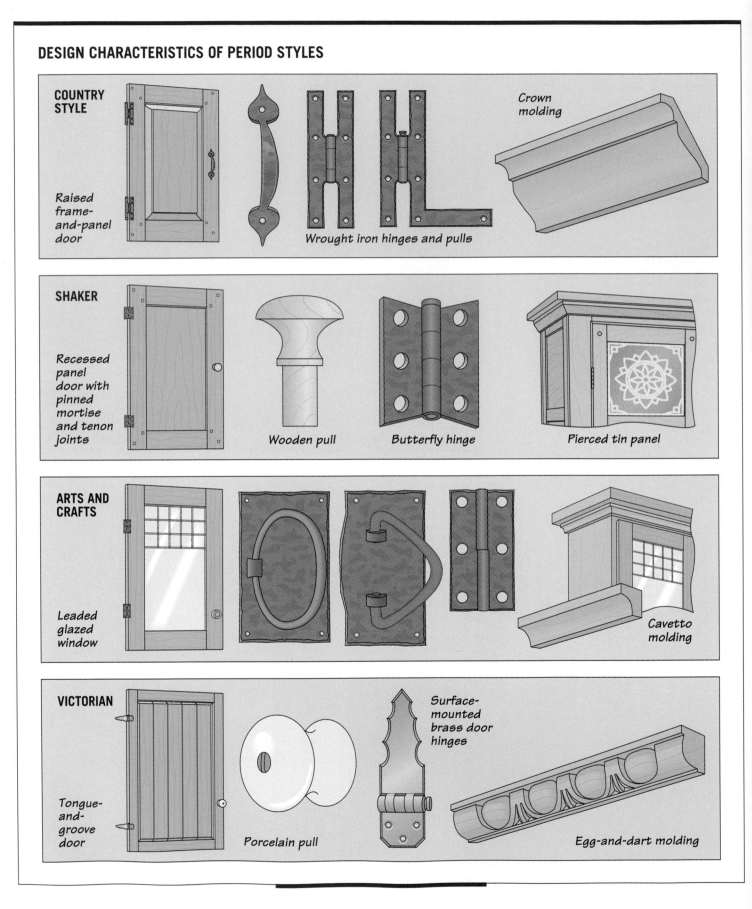

COUNTRY STYLE

Raised frame-and-panel door

Crown molding

Wrought iron hinges and pulls

SHAKER

Recessed panel door with pinned mortise and tenon joints

Wooden pull

Butterfly hinge

Pierced tin panel

ARTS AND CRAFTS

Leaded glazed window

Cavetto molding

VICTORIAN

Tongue-and-groove door

Porcelain pull

Surface-mounted brass door hinges

Egg-and-dart molding

PRINCIPLES OF LAYOUT

A successful kitchen depends on three things: sufficient space to work, adequate lighting over the sink and cooking areas, and cabinets arranged so that everything from the cutlery to the breadbox is at hand. Sometimes the area destined for the kitchen is woefully inadequate in the first of these three needs. Still, with a little creative planning, a functional kitchen can be laid out in the tightest of spaces.

The cornerstone of kitchen layout is positioning the stove, refrigerator, and sink so they form a triangle *(below)*. The smaller the triangle, the more efficient the use of space. As the illustrations on page 18 show, there are several layout options for a kitchen. The most popular of these, the U- and L-shaped designs, allow for efficient work triangles. A large kitchen can benefit from the addition of an island, which tightens the work triangle while freeing up counter space. Conversely, a single wall or corridor-style layout makes the best use of a small space.

All appliances and fixtures come with dimensional requirements of their own that should be taken into consideration before their positions are fixed. For example, a sink should have counter space of about 30 inches on each side for washing dishes; a stove should have 20 to 24 inches of space on both sides for uncluttered and safe cooking. The doors of refrigerators, dishwashers, and ovens create further demand for space; these appliances should be positioned fully open.

WORK TRIANGLES

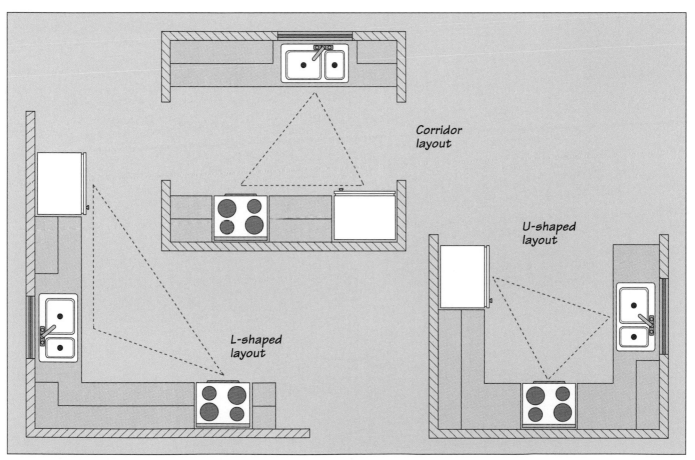

Corridor layout

U-shaped layout

L-shaped layout

Laying out an efficient kitchen

The three diagrams shown above demonstrate how to apply the principle of the work triangle for three different kitchen layouts. For maximum efficiency, the perimeter of the triangle should not exceed 25 feet; less than 20 feet is ideal. Plan your layout by first drawing your kitchen to scale, then sketch in the appliances in different arrangements until you come up with an efficient and satisfactory use of space. If possible, lay out the kitchen so the work triangles are clear of household traffic. For further ease of movement, make sure there is at least 36 inches of clearance around any peninsula or island.

A SELECTION OF KITCHEN LAYOUT OPTIONS

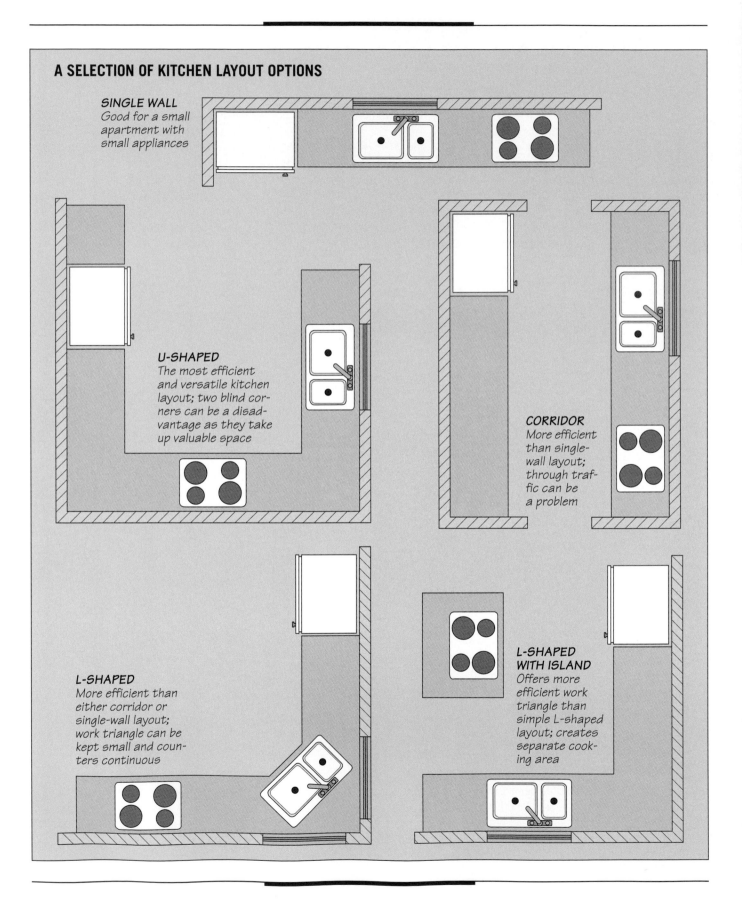

SINGLE WALL
Good for a small apartment with small appliances

U-SHAPED
The most efficient and versatile kitchen layout; two blind corners can be a disadvantage as they take up valuable space

CORRIDOR
More efficient than single-wall layout; through traffic can be a problem

L-SHAPED
More efficient than either corridor or single-wall layout; work triangle can be kept small and counters continuous

L-SHAPED WITH ISLAND
Offers more efficient work triangle than simple L-shaped layout; creates separate cooking area

DIMENSIONING

Standard measurements for kitchen cabinets are derived from human anatomy. For example, countertops are comfortable for most users when they are waist-high—typically, three feet off the floor. Subtracting four-and-a-half inches for a kickplate and one-and-a-half inches for the countertop leaves a 30-inch-high cabinet.

Upper cabinets are usually shallower than bottom ones for easier access to the countertop. A general rule of thumb for upper cabinets is to position the bottom of the lowest cabinet at shoulder height. This will fluctuate to allow for a range hood over the stove or for mounting appliances that used to crowd the countertop, such as microwaves. You can also leave a few inches beneath the cabinets to accommodate lighting. Allow for an inch or two at the top of the ceiling to add molding.

Once you have determined the height and depth of cabinets, you can start dividing the runs on your floor plan and elevations into individual cases with face frames, doors, and drawers (*page 22*). Start by positioning the sink and any other major appliances in the run, then divide the remainder of the run into cabinets. Depending on your kitchen needs, these cabinets can be large or small, with one or two doors; they could also consist of a bank of drawers. For visual balance and ease of production, try to make the cabinets proportional, so the width of a large, two-door cabinet is twice that of a smaller, one-door cabinet; 30-38 inches is a good width to work with for a large cabinet. Also take care to match the upper and lower runs. For sample floor plans and elevations of an L-shaped kitchen, see pages 20-21.

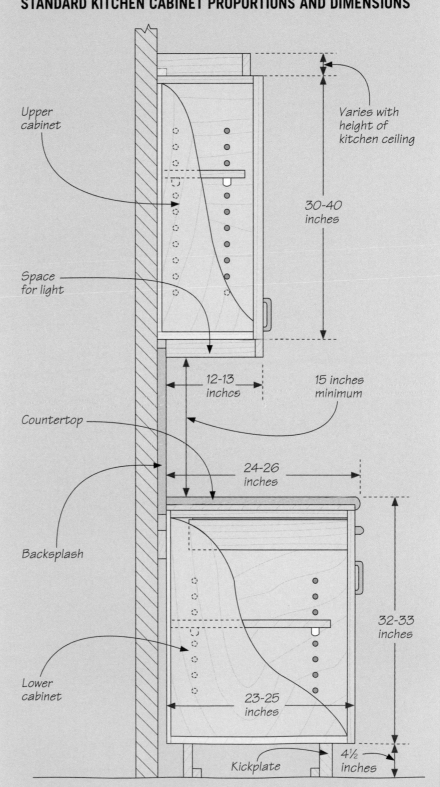

STANDARD KITCHEN CABINET PROPORTIONS AND DIMENSIONS

Upper cabinet

Varies with height of kitchen ceiling

30-40 inches

Space for light

12-13 inches

15 inches minimum

Countertop

24-26 inches

Backsplash

32-33 inches

Lower cabinet

23-25 inches

Kickplate

4½ inches

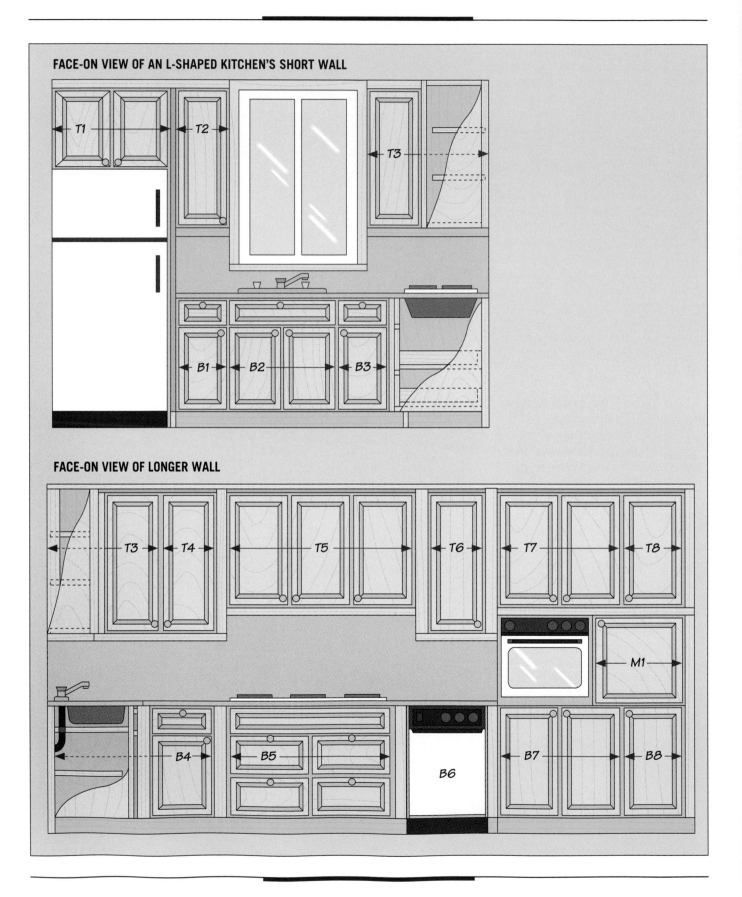

FACE-ON VIEW OF AN L-SHAPED KITCHEN'S SHORT WALL

FACE-ON VIEW OF LONGER WALL

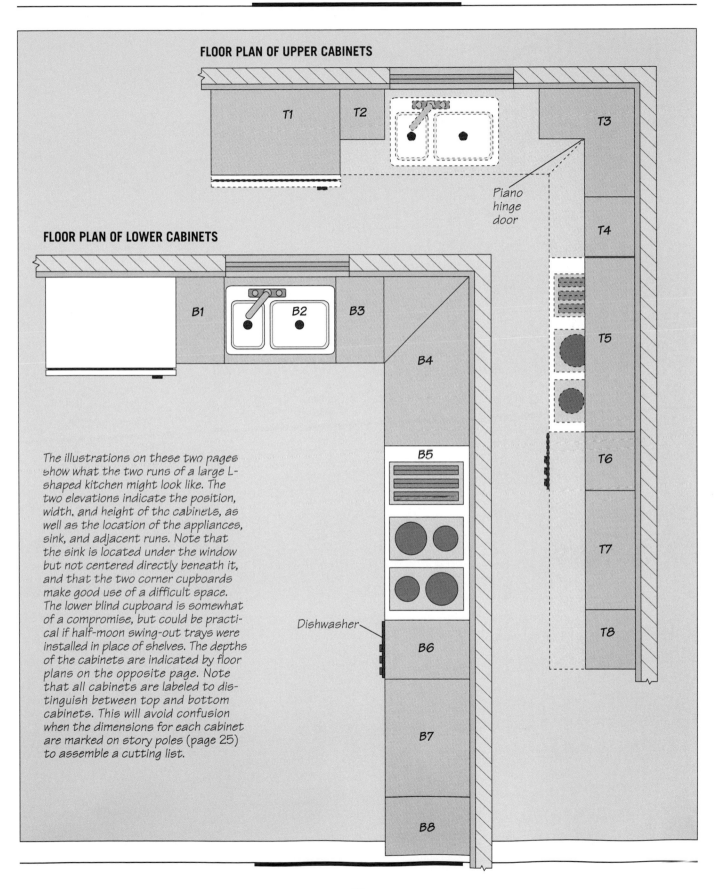

FLOOR PLAN OF UPPER CABINETS

T1

T2

T3

T4

T5

T6

T7

T8

Piano hinge door

FLOOR PLAN OF LOWER CABINETS

B1

B2

B3

B4

B5

B6

B7

B8

Dishwasher

The illustrations on these two pages show what the two runs of a large L-shaped kitchen might look like. The two elevations indicate the position, width, and height of the cabinets, as well as the location of the appliances, sink, and adjacent runs. Note that the sink is located under the window but not centered directly beneath it, and that the two corner cupboards make good use of a difficult space. The lower blind cupboard is somewhat of a compromise, but could be practical if half-moon swing-out trays were installed in place of shelves. The depths of the cabinets are indicated by floor plans on the opposite page. Note that all cabinets are labeled to distinguish between top and bottom cabinets. This will avoid confusion when the dimensions for each cabinet are marked on story poles (page 25) to assemble a cutting list.

DIVIDING A RUN

The illustration below shows how to divide a lower and upper run of cabinets. In the lower run, the dishwasher and sink are positioned, then the rest of the run is divided into equal cases. Next, the cases are divided into drawers and doors. In this example, the upper cabinet run is also divided to match the lower run. For different matching effects, see the illustration at the bottom of the page.

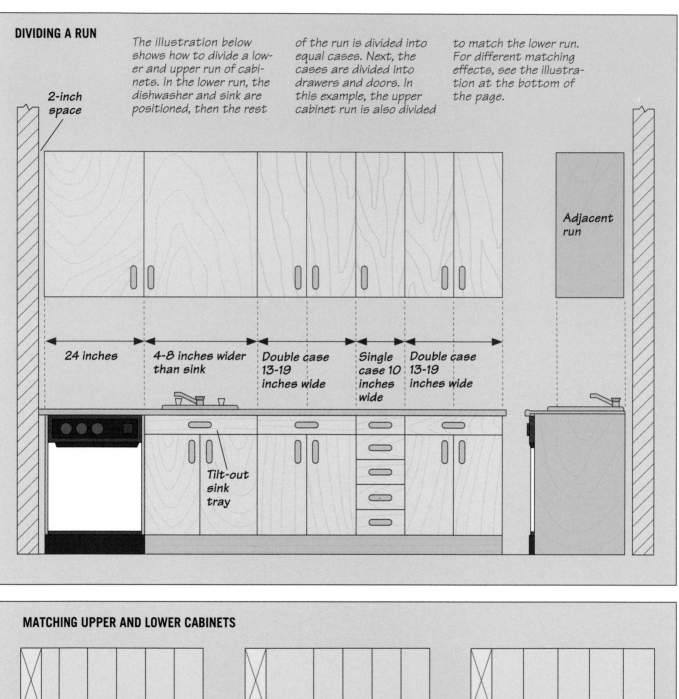

2-inch space

Adjacent run

24 inches

4-8 inches wider than sink

Double case 13-19 inches wide

Single case 10 inches wide

Double case 13-19 inches wide

Tilt-out sink tray

MATCHING UPPER AND LOWER CABINETS

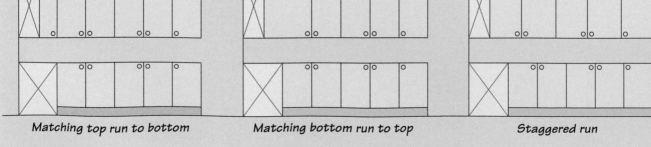

Matching top run to bottom

Matching bottom run to top

Staggered run

STORY POLES

S tory poles are a method of measuring kitchen cabinets accurately for a master cutting list without relying on a tape measure or ruler. Carpenters have been laying out entire homes on these long, narrow sticks of wood for centuries, and this tried-and-true method offers several advantages over standard measuring techniques. For one, all measurements are marked out full-size, making an error-free cutting list easier to calculate than from scale drawings.

Story poles also allow you to visualize construction details more easily. By marking the measurements for each cabinet on the sticks you have an exact picture of each cabinet; lengths, widths, and positions of joints can all be marked later on the stock directly, without a tape measure introducing error. For ease of handling, make your story poles from wood 1/4 inch to 3/4 inch thick and about 1 1/2 inches wide. To see the pencil marks better, use light-colored wood.

When laying out a kitchen, site story poles are first completed for each wall of the kitchen *(page 24)*. On the horizontal story pole, the location of everything along that wall is marked: the appliances and cabinets in the run, doors, windows, and any electrical or plumbing fixtures such as outlets or sink pipes *(see photo, page 13)*. The vertical story pole shows the height of the kickplate, lower cabinet, countertop, backsplash, upper cabinet, and ceiling molding, as well as any windows and electrical or plumbing fixtures. A depth story pole provides the depth of kickplate, cabinet, and countertop overhang.

Once the kitchen has been laid out on story poles, individual story poles are created for each cabinet *(page 25)*. For maximum accuracy, each cabinet should have three smaller story poles: height, width, and depth, each referenced to the respective site story pole. These shorter story poles will tell you the dimensions of your cabinets *(right)* when it comes time to compile the master cutting list *(page 32)*.

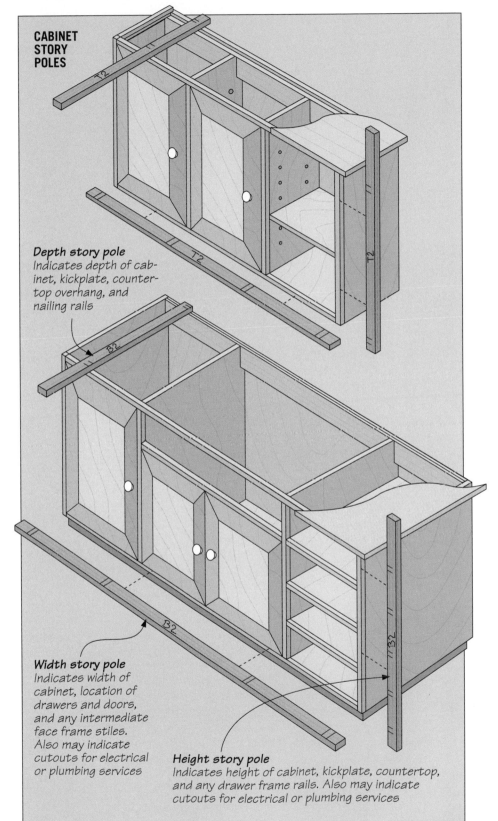

CABINET STORY POLES

Depth story pole
Indicates depth of cabinet, kickplate, countertop overhang, and nailing rails

Width story pole
Indicates width of cabinet, location of drawers and doors, and any intermediate face frame stiles. Also may indicate cutouts for electrical or plumbing services

Height story pole
Indicates height of cabinet, kickplate, countertop, and any drawer frame rails. Also may indicate cutouts for electrical or plumbing services

LAYING OUT A KITCHEN WITH STORY POLES

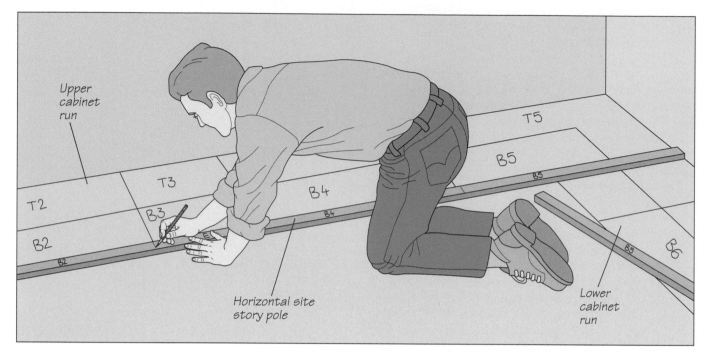

Upper cabinet run

T5

B5

T3

B4

T2

B3

B2

B4

B5

B6

Horizontal site story pole

Lower cabinet run

1 Making horizontal site poles

Using chalk, sketch a full-size outline of your kitchen layout on the site floor. Mark both the upper and lower cabinet runs, indicating which cases will be cabinets and which will be appliances. Then create a horizontal site story pole for each wall in the kitchen. On the pole, mark the location of all cabinets in both runs *(above)* and any doors or windows. If the kitchen wall is unusually long, you can join two sticks together to span the distance.

2 Making vertical site poles

Floors and ceilings are often not flat or level, so you need to know the minimum distance between the two to plan the height of your cabinets. Strike a level reference line on the walls around the kitchen. Then find the high point of the floor and hold the vertical site story pole at this point, plumb to the reference line. Set a compass to the height of the kickplate and mark this point on the story pole *(right)*. Use the compass to make a similar mark to record the height of any molding at the top of the pole. Now mark the height of the upper and lower cabinets on the vertical pole, as well as the location of any windows on that wall. Lastly, create a depth story pole for the wall indicating the depth of the cabinets and any other features on the wall adjacent to the run.

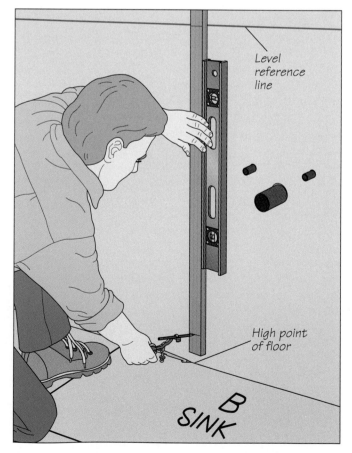

Level reference line

High point of floor

B SINK

3 Locating electrical and plumbing services

Use a carpenter's level to draw plumb lines from the location of any plumbing or electrical services to the level reference line *(right)*. Transfer these locations to the horizontal and vertical site story poles for the run.

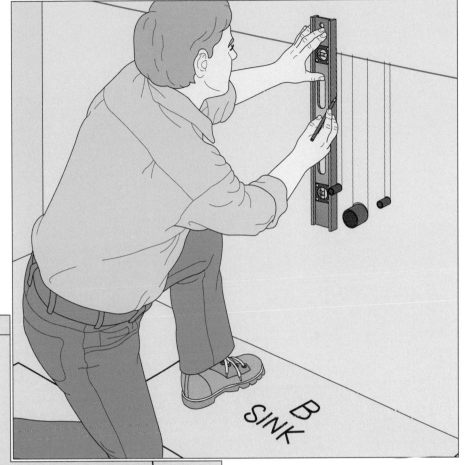

SINK B

T3 DRAWERS

B3 DRAWERS

Horizontal cabinet story pole

← SIDE | B3 DRAWERS | SIDE →

FACE FRAME

Horizontal site pole | B3 DRAWERS

4 Creating cabinet story poles

Make horizontal, vertical, and depth story poles for each cabinet, then reference each to its respective site pole for the run the cabinet is in. In the example shown at left, the horizontal story pole for a bank of drawers is being referenced to its horizontal site pole. Mark out the details of the cabinet—in this case, the face frame rails and stiles—within the cabinet width. On the vertical story pole, mark the height of the kickplate, countertop, backsplash, upper cabinet, and ceiling molding, as well as any windows and electrical or plumbing services. Mark the depth of kickplate, cabinet, and countertop overhang on the depth pole. Be sure to label all poles carefully to avoid confusion later.

CASEWORK

An appliance bay is a tidy way to keep a countertop free of clutter. Blenders, coffee makers, toasters, and other small appliances can be kept out of sight but readily accessible. While the appliance bay shown above features louvered doors, space can be saved by using tambour doors (page 40).

Built-in kitchen cabinets are relatively recent arrivals in domestic kitchens. Traditionally, kitchen cupboards were freestanding units with frame-and-panel construction and face frames, much like the china cabinet in the parlor. Yet by the turn of the century, the switch to built-ins had already begun. It accelerated during the post-WW II housing boom in Europe, when the construction of millions of new homes prompted the development of new wood products, tools, and techniques that saved labor and materials. No room in the house benefitted from these advances more than the kitchen.

The development of plywood, particleboard, fiberboard, and other manufactured sheet goods made assembly-line production of large and rigid cabinets possible. The European 32-millimeter system—so called because all the holes for drawer slides, dowels, shelf supports, and hinges are spaced 32 millimeters apart—was revolutionary in design. Its modular, predrilled melamine cabinets offered unparalleled flexibility. It also made the modern kitchen affordable: Even the most modest home could now be outfitted with a full complement of sleek kitchen cabinets.

Building these cases is mainly a matter of cutting the stock to size and then joining it using one of the techniques shown on pages 33 to 37; the chart on page 31 will help you choose from available materials. Face frames, doors, drawer fronts, and other hardware can then be added to create an appropriate style.

While the wide availability of materials such as medium density fiberboard has simplified casework, sheet goods still have an Achilles' heel: their edges are unattractive and need to be hidden. Laminate board can be edged with hardwood strips *(page 48)* or laminate edge banding *(page 49)*. The traditional face frame *(page 50)*, a solid-wood frame consisting of rails and stiles that is attached to the front of the finished case, is another way to hide the edges of man-made boards. More importantly, the face frame can impart a traditional, handcrafted feel to the kitchen.

Shelving and storage are key considerations in casework construction. For example, a bank of graduated drawers—the ideal solution for cutlery and kitchen utensils—should not be an afterthought if you are using face frames on your cabinets. (For more on drawers, see chapter three.) Adjustable shelves *(page 38)* can add flexibility to your cabinets, enabling you to store oversized bulk goods and adapt to changing culinary needs. They are also simple to install if you drill the support holes before assembling the cases. Another modern storage idea, the lazy Susan *(page 42)*, makes good use of a perennial weak spot in the kitchen: the lower corner cupboard. An appliance bay *(photo above and page 40)* is a separate piece of casework in its own right.

Accurately cutting sheet goods to size can be a tricky task. In the photo at left, a panel-cutting circular saw attachment is being used to rip a sheet of melamine for a kitchen cabinet. The Exact-T-Guide model shown features a T-square-type guide that rides in a U-shaped channel screwed to the edge of a plywood base.

ANATOMY OF A KITCHEN CABINET CASE

Kitchen cabinets should be kept as basic as possible. Using sheet goods *(page 31)* and simple joinery techniques will keep the time and expense of building and installing a kitchen's worth of cabinets to a minimum. Although their construction is simple, it is important that the cases be well-built. Drawers, doors, and countertops will all be easier to fit if the casework is strong, straight, and square. Spending a little extra time in the building stage will save much frustration during installation.

The anatomies below and on the facing page show basic cabinet construction. Use the measurements from your cabinet story poles *(page 25)* to cut the stock for each cabinet to size. The sides of the bottom cabinet can extend right down to the floor, or you can install leveler legs *(page 44)* that will hold a clip-on kickplate. At this time, it is a good idea to cut all the grooves for the back panels, and to bore holes for any adjustable shelving *(page 38)*.

If you are after a traditional look, solid-wood face frames can be added after the cabinets are built. If you do not choose face frames, the exposed edge of the plywood must be covered with some sort of banding, either laminate or solid wood. While there are many ways to join boards, efficiency favors certain methods. Biscuit, lock miter, tongue-and-groove joints and ready-to-assemble—or RTA—fasteners, can all be used to produce joints that combine ease of installation with accuracy and strength.

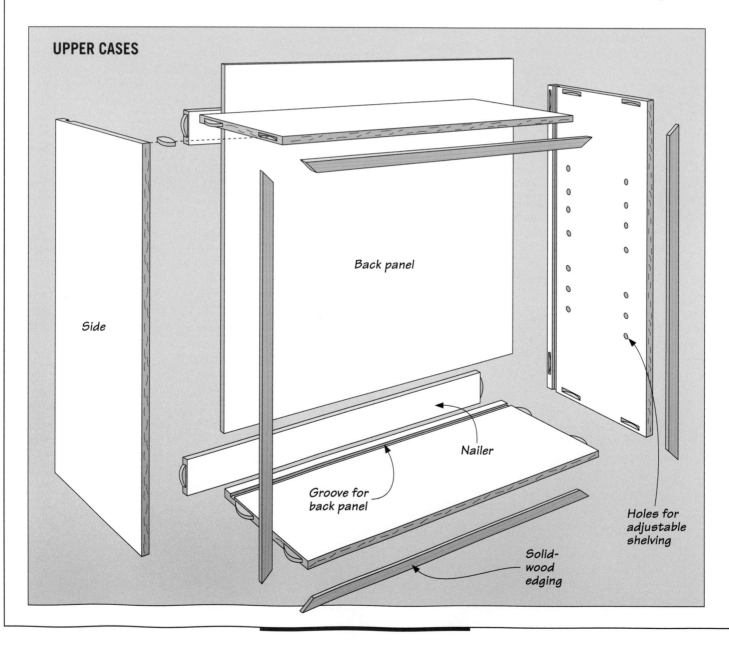

UPPER CASES

Back panel

Side

Nailer

Groove for back panel

Holes for adjustable shelving

Solid-wood edging

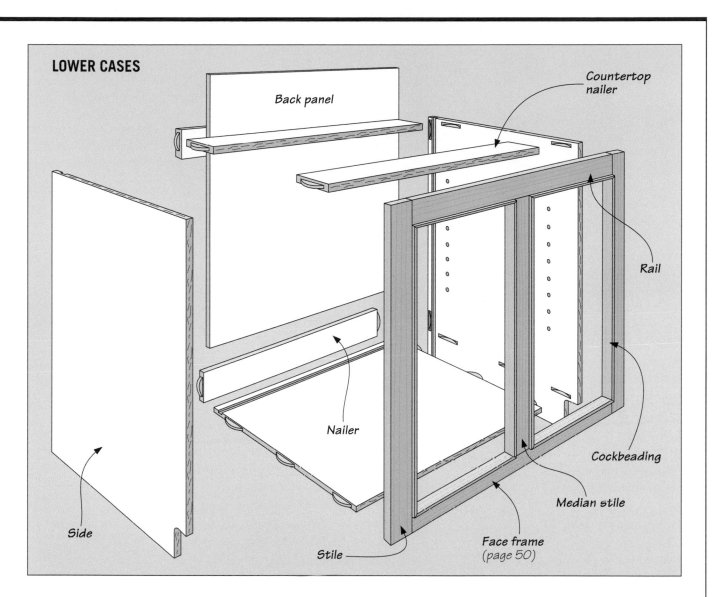

LOWER CASES

Back panel

Countertop nailer

Rail

Cockbeading

Median stile

Side

Nailer

Stile

Face frame
(page 50)

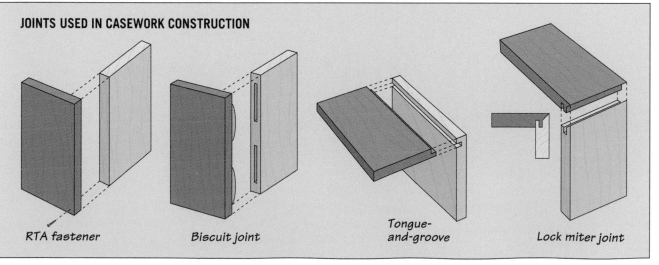

JOINTS USED IN CASEWORK CONSTRUCTION

RTA fastener

Biscuit joint

Tongue-and-groove

Lock miter joint

BUILDING MATERIALS

Traditionally, all cabinets were built entirely of solid wood. But close examination of antique furniture can offer an instructive surprise. Yesterday's woodworkers often used less attractive woods like poplar and pine for hidden parts such as drawer sides and cabinet

From the economical to the expensive, a vast array of sheet goods is available for use in casework. The photo at left shows a selection of sheet goods, including samples of melamine-coated particle board, medium density fiberboard, and veneered plywood.

backs; there was no point in putting walnut and cherry where it would never be seen. Today, cabinetmakers still save the cherry and walnut for the drawer fronts, but they rely on man-made sheet goods for the insides of the cabinets. Not only do they save money and conserve resources, but sheet goods also outperform wood in terms of dimensional stability.

The chart below offers an overview of different materials used in making kitchen cabinets, from melamine to plywood to solid wood. Each has its own strengths and weaknesses. The challenge is to choose the best product for each component and for the style of your cabinets.

CASEWORK MATERIALS

MATERIAL	RELATIVE COST	CHARACTERISTICS
CABINET-GRADE PLYWOOD (softwood veneer core)		
Rotary cut hardwood veneer	Moderate	Easy to work, very strong and dimensionally stable; face veneer not as attractive as plainsawn variety. Edges must be faced with solid wood; needs little sanding.
Plainsawn veneer	High	Same as above but face veneer resembles edge-joined boards.
SOLID WOOD		
Cherry	Moderate	One of the finest cabinet woods. Reddish-brown color darkens with age; finegrained texture accepts natural finishes well. Moderately difficult to work; resins in the wood can leave burn marks.
Oak, ash	Moderate to low	Strong, stable hardwoods with prominent, open grain; accepts natural finishes well.
Maple, birch	Moderate to low	Straight-grained, stable hardwoods that provide a smooth finish. Density can make these woods difficult to work; maple in particular can blunt tools.
Walnut	Moderate to high	Choice cabinet wood with rich color and grain; easily worked with all hand and power tools; accepts natural finishes well.
Pine, poplar, alder	Low	Much softer than above woods, yet just as stable. Easy to work but also easily damaged. Very little figure; typically finished with paint.
COMPOSITE		
Medium density fiberboard (MDF)	Moderate	Strong and dimensionally stable; edges easy to rout, shape, or groove; available with plywood face veneers. Can be finished or painted with little or no sanding. Some varieties can emit toxic fumes when sawn; use of carbide-tipped tools is recommended.
Particleboard	Low	Slightly less strong and stable than MDF; holds fasteners poorly. More difficult to work and finish; available with plywood face veneers.
Melamine	Moderate	Common term for plywood or particle board surfaced with a hard plastic laminate; comes in a variety of colors. Tough and long-lasting; only as strong as its substrate.

TYPES OF PLYWOOD

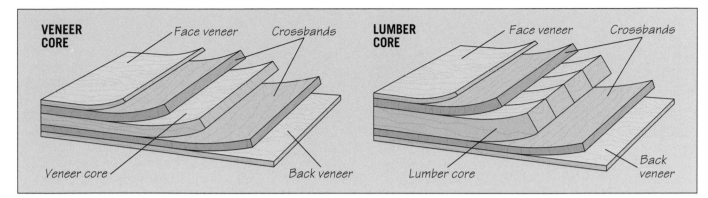

Types of plywood

The basic design of all plywood is the same: a core covered on both sides by layers of crossbanding and a face veneer. The most common type has a veneer core. All softwood plywoods are made this way, and they are stable, warp-resistant, and inexpensive. Hardwood plywoods can also be made with solid lumber or particleboard cores. The middle ply of lumber-core plywood consists of several narrow strips of solid wood—usually mahogany, poplar, or basswood—edge-glued together. Particleboard-core plywood has a solid core of particleboard or medium density fiberboard. Lumber-core plywood holds nails and screws best and is preferable where additional strength and flatness are required. "Cabinet-quality" plywoods with superior face veneers are recommended for visible surfaces such as doors and drawer faces. There are two broad categories of cabinet-quality plywood: rotary sawn and plainsawn. While equal in strength, plainsawn plywood can resemble a glued-up solid wood panel, while rotary sawn veneer is easily identified as plywood.

PLYWOOD FACE VENEER GRADES

HARDWOOD PLYWOOD	
Premium	Face veneer with well-matched seams and smooth surface; made of specific hardwood, such as walnut or mahogany. Even color and grain
Good	Face veneer similar to premium, but not as well matched. Free of sharp contrasts in color and grain
Sound	Face veneer smooth, but not matched for color or grain; defects only on back veneer. Generally intended for painting
Utility	Veneers have rough grain and may have knotholes up to ¾ inch, as well as some discoloration, staining, and slight splits. Not matched for color or grain
Back	May have larger defects than utility grade, but none that impair panel strength. Not matched for color or grain
Specialty	Made to order to meet specific requirements, such as separate panels with matching grain patterns

SOFTWOOD PLYWOOD	
N	Sanded smooth; can take a clear finish; face veneer matched for grain and color, free of open defects
A	Sanded smooth; can take a natural finish, but is more often painted
B	Smooth and sanded; may have minor splits
C	Smooth; may have some broken grain, sanding defects and knotholes up to ¾ inch
C Plugged	Sanded; similar to C grade, but knotholes and splits are smaller
D	Used mainly for inner plies and back veneer; may have knot holes up to 2½ inches

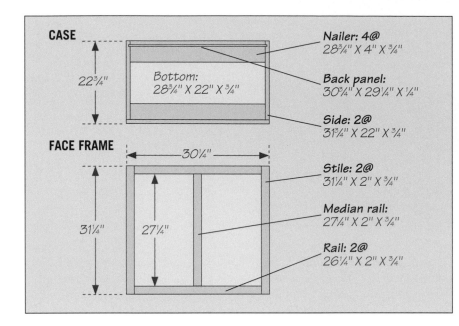

CASE

22¾"

Bottom:
28¾" X 22" X ¾"

Nailer: 4@
28¾" X 4" X ¾"

Back panel:
30¾" X 29¼" X ¼"

Side: 2@
31¼" X 22" X ¾"

FACE FRAME

30¼"

31¼"   27¼"

Stile: 2@
31¼" X 2" X ¾"

Median rail:
27¼" X 2" X ¾"

Rail: 2@
26¼" X 2" X ¾"

Making a cutting list

Making a master cutting list for a kitchen full of cabinets may seem like a daunting task, yet if you have been scrupulous about marking accurate story poles for all your cabinets, then deducing a cutting list is relatively straightforward. Write a separate cutting list for each cabinet on an index card *(left)*. Make a rough sketch of the cabinet and jot down a list of all the components and materials, taking their measurements from the cabinet's story poles *(page 25)*. To avoid confusion later on, make sure to label the card the same as your cabinet. The master cutting list can then be calculated based on the requirements listed on all the cards. To speed things up at the lumberyard, you may wish to create separate master lists for solid stock and sheet stock.

ESTIMATING BOARD FEET

CALCULATING BOARD FEET

Ordering lumber by the board foot

The "board foot" is a unit of measurement used to calculate the volume of a given amount of stock. It is commonly used with hardwood lumber. As shown in the illustration at right, the standard board foot is equivalent to a piece that is 1 inch thick, 12 inches wide, and 12 inches long. To calculate the number of board feet in a piece of wood, multiply its three dimensions together. Then, divide the result by 144 if the dimensions are in inches, or by 12 if just one dimension is in feet.

The formula for a standard board:
1" x 12" x 12" ÷ 144 = 1
(or 1" x 12" x 1' ÷ 12 = 1)
So, if you had a 6-foot-long plank that is 1 inch thick and 4 inches wide, you would calculate the board feet as follows: 1" x 4" x 6' ÷ 12 = 2 (or 2 board feet). Other examples are shown in the illustration. Remember that board feet are calculated on the basis of the nominal rather than actual dimensions of the stock; consequently, the board feet contained in a 2-by-4 that actually measures 1½-by-3½ inches would be calculated using the larger dimensions.

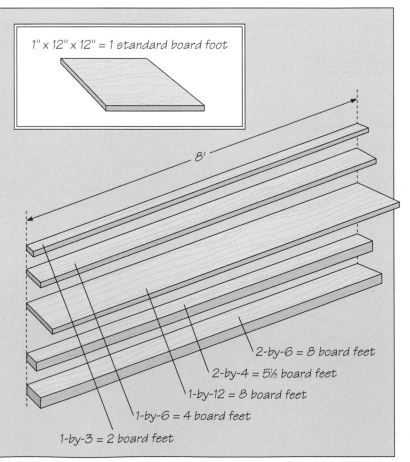

1" x 12" x 12" = 1 standard board foot

8'

2-by-6 = 8 board feet

2-by-4 = 5⅓ board feet

1-by-12 = 8 board feet

1-by-6 = 4 board feet

1-by-3 = 2 board feet

BUILDING THE CASES

After you have calculated a master cutting list for your cabinets, you are finally ready to start building them. As you cut the materials to size, carefully mark each piece to indicate which cabinet it belongs to. Then cut the grooves for the back panels and bore the holes for any adjustable shelving *(page 38)*.

With this groundwork done, assembly is largely a matter of choosing a joinery method. If you are comfortable with your table saw, tongue-and-groove joints *(page 35)* are a good choice. Those well-versed in using a plate jointer may want to join their cases with biscuits *(below)*, a joint equal in strength to the tongue-and-groove. If you have a shaper or a very solid router table and a heavy-duty router, lock miter joints *(page 36)* are solid, durable, and easy to cut. If space in your workshop is at a premium or if you need to disassemble and move your cabinets, ready-to-assemble —or RTA—fasteners *(page 37)* may be the best choice.

Cutting sheet goods such as melamine on the table saw often results in rough edges, chipping, and tearout. Installed on a table saw's arbor, the Modulus scoring saw attachment shown above features a smaller blade that cleanly scores the sheet before the main blade cuts it, resulting in a professional, smooth cut.

JOINING CASES WITH BISCUITS

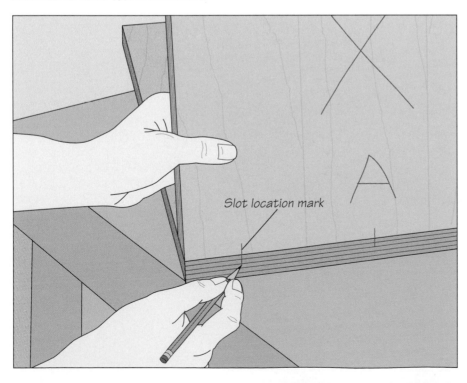

Slot location mark

1 Marking the slot locations
For each cabinet, identify the outside face of all four panels with an X, then mark location lines for the biscuit slots on each of the four corners. (On lower cabinets, which typically do not have a top panel, mark the location lines between the countertop nailers and the side panels.) To start, place one side panel outside-face down on a work surface and hold the top panel at a 90° angle to it. Use a pencil to mark lines on the adjoining panels about 2 inches in from each corner *(left)*. Mark additional lines about every 4 to 6 inches. Repeat to mark slot locations on the other three corners of the case. Add reference letters to help you identify the corners.

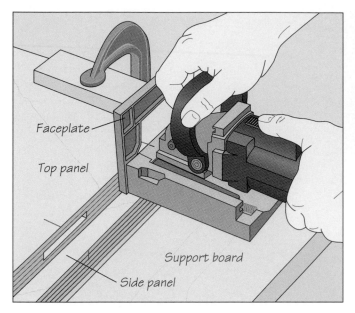

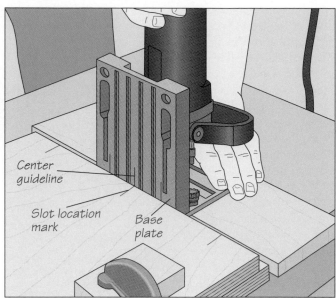

2 Cutting the slots

The setup shown above will allow you to cut the slots for one mating corner of the case without moving the panels. Place a side panel of the case outside-face down on a work surface, then set the top panel outside-face up on top. Offset the top panel from the edge of the side panel by the stock thickness and clamp the panels in place; make sure the mating slot location marks on the two pieces of stock are perfectly aligned. Set the proper depth of cut on the plate joiner following the manu-

facturer's instructions. To cut the slots in the top panel, butt the tool's faceplate against the end of the top panel, aligning the guideline on the faceplate with a slot location mark and resting the tool on a support board the same thickness as the stock. Cut a slot at each mark *(above, left)*. To cut the mating slots in the side panel, butt the joiner's base plate against the top panel and align the center guideline on the plate with a slot location mark *(above, right)*.

3 Cutting slots for a partition

Vertical partitions or fixed shelves between case sides can also be joined with biscuits. Use a framing square to lay out the thickness of the partition on the mating panels, then lay the partition atop one of the panels with its lower edge aligned with the layout line. Clamp the assembly to a work surface. Cut the slots in the panel and partition as in step 2 above. Repeat to make the slots at the other end of the partition and the second mating panel *(right)*. Since some plate joiners cut slots slightly off center, keep the same side of the partition face-up for both cuts.

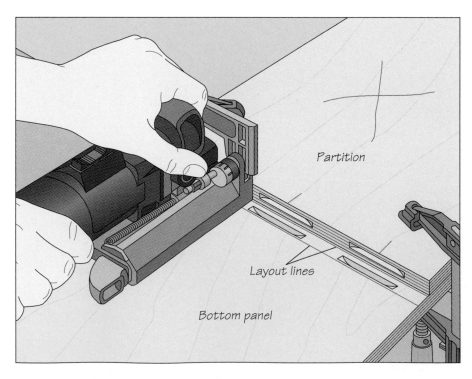

JOINING CASES WITH TONGUE-AND-GROOVE JOINTS

1 Setting up the table saw
Use a dado head on a table saw to cut grooves in the side panels and tongues in the top and bottom panels. Cut the grooves first. Install a dado head set to half the thickness of the stock, and attach an auxiliary wood fence to support the workpiece during the cut. Butting a side panel against the fence as shown, slide the rip fence toward the blade until the outside face of the workpiece is in line with the edge of the saw blade *(right)*. Lastly, set the blade height equal to half the thickness of the stock.

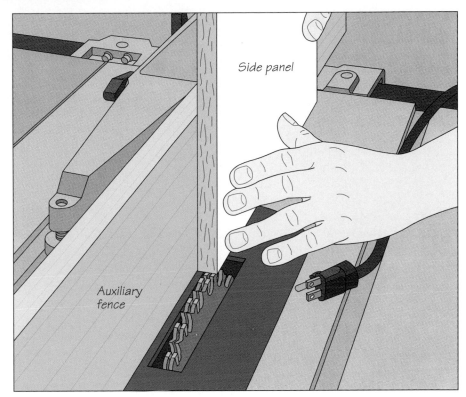

Side panel

Auxiliary fence

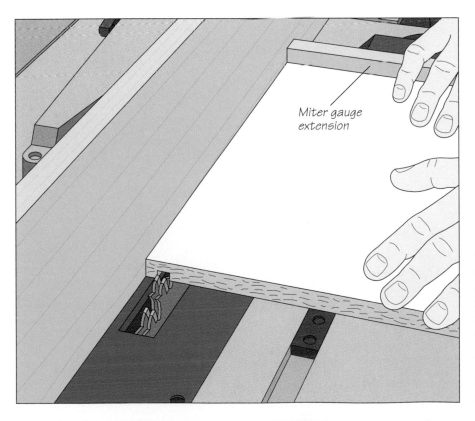

Miter gauge extension

2 Cutting the groove
Lay the side panel inside-face down on the saw table and butt its top end against the auxiliary wood fence. Use the miter gauge equipped with an extension to feed the panel into the blades *(left)*, pressing the workpiece against the fence throughout the cut. Keep your hands well away from the blades. Repeat the cut for the bottom end of the panel.

35

3 Cutting the tongues

To cut tongues in the top and bottom panels, first unplug the saw and add a spacer to the dado head. Lower the blades below the table surface and move the auxiliary wood fence so it overlaps the cutters slightly. Turn on the saw and raise the dado head to cut a notch in the auxiliary fence. Set the height of the dado head and its width of cut equal to half the stock thickness. With the top panel outside-face up on the table saw, butt one side against the fence. Feed the panel into the cutters *(right)*, applying slight pressure toward the fence throughout the operation. Repeat for the other side of the top panel and the bottom panel.

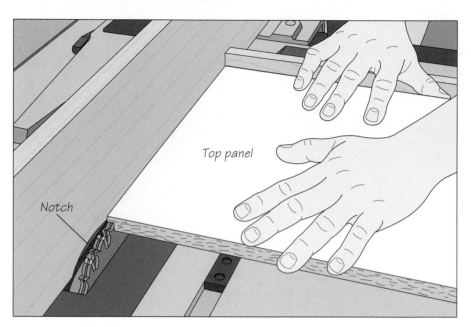

Top panel

Notch

JOINING CASES WITH A LOCK MITER JOINT

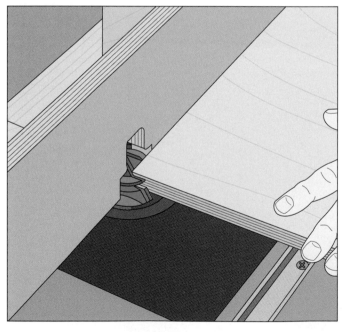

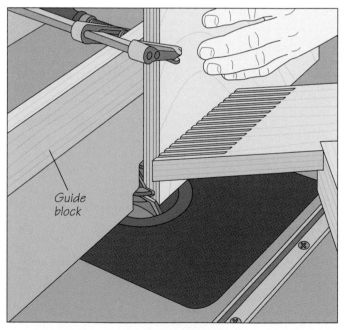

Guide block

Making the cuts

Install a lock miter bit in your router and mount the tool in a table. Attach a notched auxiliary fence and screw an extension to the miter gauge. Set the bit height so the uppermost cutter is centered on the end of the panel with the panel flat on the table. Position the auxiliary fence so the bit will miter the stock without shortening it. Next, make test cuts in two pieces of plywood scrap the same thickness as your panels. Butting one

piece of scrap against the fence and the miter gauge extension, feed it into the bit *(above, left)*. To cut the mating piece, clamp a guide block to it to ride atop the fence. Then feed the board on end into the bit *(above, right)*, keeping it flush against the fence with one hand while pushing it and the guide block forward with the other. Test the fit and adjust the position of the fence as necessary before making the cuts in the case panels.

USING READY-TO-ASSEMBLE FASTENERS

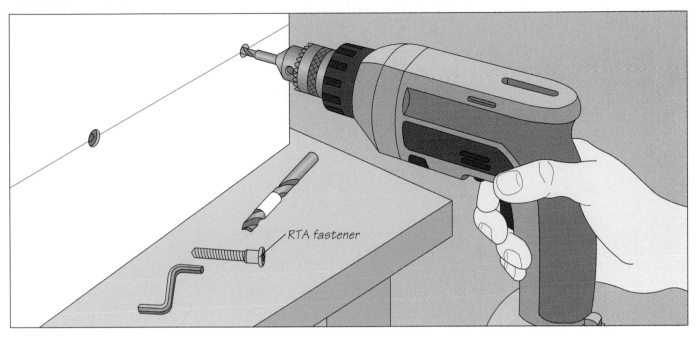

RTA fastener

1 Preparing the holes

To join a case with ready-to-assemble or RTA fasteners, first dry assemble the finished case and secure it squarely with clamps *(page 47)*. To help position the fasteners, draw lines on the sides of the case indicating the center of the top and bottom panels. (In the example shown, the bottom of the case is set 4 inches from the floor.) While special stepped drill bits are available to bore the pilot holes and countersink them in a single step, a simple alternative is to use two different-sized bits. Start with a bit slightly wider than the base of the fastener; wrap a length of tape around the bit to mark the desired depth—slightly more than the length of the fastener base. Drill a series of countersink holes to the appropriate depth, spacing the holes about 5 inches apart. Then install a bit slightly smaller than the fastener shank to drill the pilot holes. Mark the appropriate depth with masking tape, then bore the holes *(above)*.

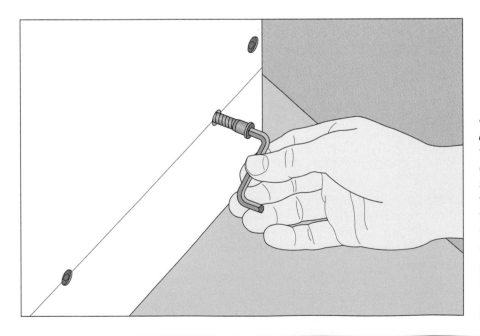

2 Installing the fasteners

If you wish to move your cabinets from one kitchen to another (or if your cabinets are large and you intend to disassemble them before transporting them to the installation site), simply drive a fastener in each predrilled hole *(left)*. The fasteners can be removed later and the cabinets knocked down for easy transport. If you want to install your cabinets permanently, then remove the clamps and apply glue to the mating edges of the joints before driving the fasteners.

SHELVING AND STORAGE

Cooks seldom complain about having too much storage space in their kitchens. Appliances, pots, cans, spice racks, cookbooks, and dishes all seem to conspire to fill every nook and cranny of available space. Efficient shelving and storage devices can create a surprising amount of space simply by keeping things organized. For example, the height of adjustable shelves *(below)* can be changed to accommodate different-sized dry goods or dishes. Corner cabinets are particularly prone to wasting valuable space; items at the very back of such cabinets tend to be forgotten. A lazy Susan *(page 42)* is an elegant solution to this problem: Its two round shelves rotate around a central shaft, making all the contents readily accessible.

From towel racks to slide-out garbage bins, there are many commercial storage devices on the market designed to reduce time spent rummaging in lower cabinets. The photo at left shows slide-out shelving mounted on drawer slides.

Appliance clutter is another common kitchen complaint. Certain appliances that see frequent use, such as toasters, coffee makers, and blenders, often crowd the countertop. An appliance bay with a sliding tambour door *(page 40)* provides a tidy place to keep these kitchen conveniences plugged in and out of sight, yet easily accessible.

INSTALLING ADJUSTABLE SHELF SUPPORTS

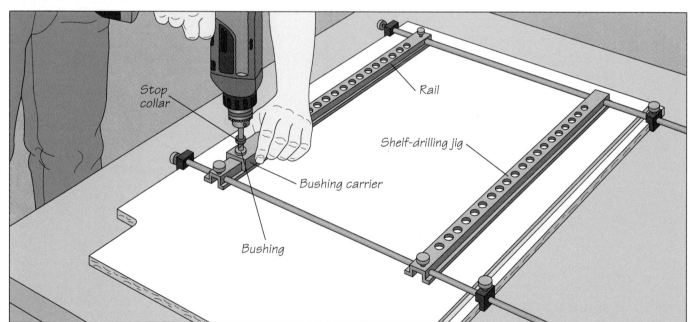

Stop collar

Rail

Shelf-drilling jig

Bushing carrier

Bushing

1 Drilling holes for the sleeves

Adjustable shelving requires two parallel rows of holes to be drilled in the side panels of the cabinet case. The commercial jig shown above allows you to bore holes at 1-inch intervals and ensures that corresponding holes will be perfectly aligned. Set a side panel inside-face up on a work surface and clamp the jig to the edges of the panel; the holes can be any distance from the panel edges, but about 2 inches in would be best for the panels shown. Fit your drill with a bit the same diameter as the sleeves and install a stop collar to mark the drilling depth equal to the sleeve length. Starting at either end of one of the jig's rails, place the appropriate bushing in the first hole of the bushing carrier. (The bushing keeps the bit perfectly square to the workpiece.) Holding the drill and carrier, bore the hole. Drill a series of evenly spaced holes along both rails. Remove the jig and repeat for the other side panel of the case, carefully positioning the jig so the holes will be aligned with those in the first panel.

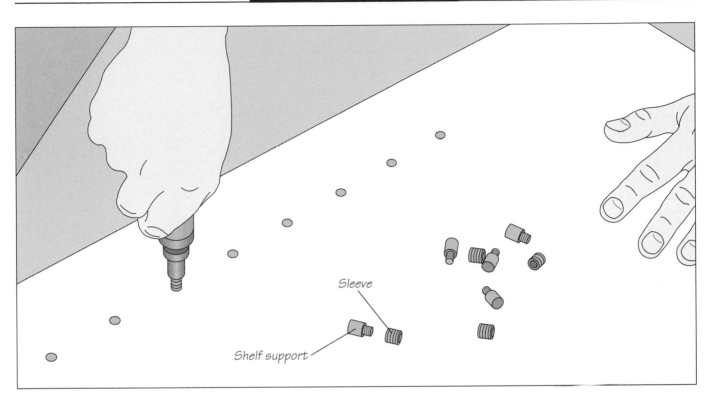

Sleeve

Shelf support

2 Mounting the sleeves and supports
To install the threaded sleeves without damaging them, use a sleeve-setting punch. Place a sleeve on the end of the punch and push the sleeve firmly into one of the holes in a side panel *(above)*. Insert a sleeve into each hole you have drilled, then screw shelf supports into the sleeves at each desired shelf location.

SHOP TIP

A shop-made shelf drilling jig
The T-shaped jig shown at right will allow you to bore a row of evenly spaced holes as accurately as a commercial jig. Make the jig from 1-by-3 stock, being careful to screw the fence and arm together at a perfect 90° angle. Mark a line down the center of the arm and bore holes along it at 2-inch intervals with the same bit you would use for threaded sleeves. To use the jig, clamp it to a side panel with the fence butted against either end of the panel and the marked centerline 2 inches in from its edge. Fit your drill bit with a stop collar, bore the holes, and reposition the jig for each new row.

BUILDING AN APPLIANCE BAY

1 Milling tambour slats

Start by cutting the tambour stock to size; make the length of the stock equal to the width of the tambour door plus ⅝ inch. Then plane the stock to a thickness equal to the desired width of the slats; typically ¾ to 1 inch. Mill the slats in three steps *(right)*. First, joint the edges of the stock *(A)*. Next, use a ¼-inch rounding over bit to shape the two long edges of the stock on your router table *(B)*. Finally, rip a ¼- to ½-inch-thick strip from each edge to make the first two slats *(C)*; use a push stick to keep your fingers away from the blade. Joint the stock again, then repeat the last two steps until you have enough slats to make the tambour door. The combined height of the slats should total 2 or 3 inches more than the height of the door opening. Trim all the slats to length.

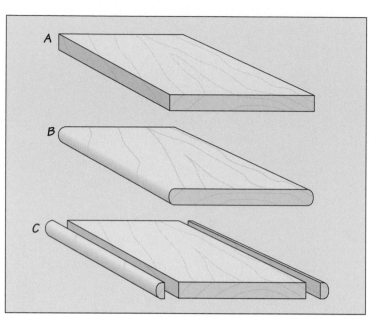

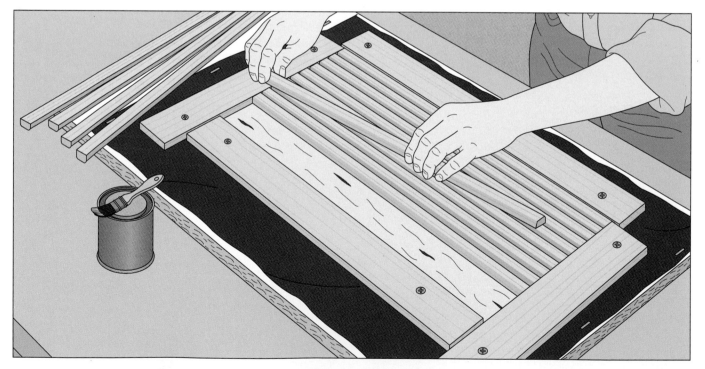

2 Gluing the slats to a backing

Use lightweight canvas as backing for the slats. Stretch the canvas over a piece of melamine and pull it taut, smoothing out all the wrinkles. Secure it in place with staples. To help align the slats, screw three boards to the plywood to form a U-shaped jig. The device should be as wide as the slats are long and perfectly square. Slide all the slats into place then screw a fourth board to close the top of the jig. Remove the slats and apply an even coat of white glue to the canvas. Glue the slats back in place *(above)*, then weight them down to get a good bond. Let the assembly dry overnight. Unscrew the jig and trim the excess canvas with a sharp knife.

3 Routing the tambour track

Starting at the bottom of the panel, draw the desired shape of the tambour door track on one of the case sides. Fashion a template that copies the inside line of this track. Place the template atop the case side, aligning it with the track's inside line. Install a top-piloted flush trimming bit in your router; the diameter of the bit should be $\frac{1}{16}$ inch greater than the thickness of the door. Set the router on the template and adjust the cutting depth to make a $\frac{3}{8}$-inch-deep groove; use shims under the pattern if necessary. Rout the track *(right)*, keeping the bearing pressed against the pattern throughout the cut. To rout the tambour track in the opposite case side, turn the pattern over and repeat.

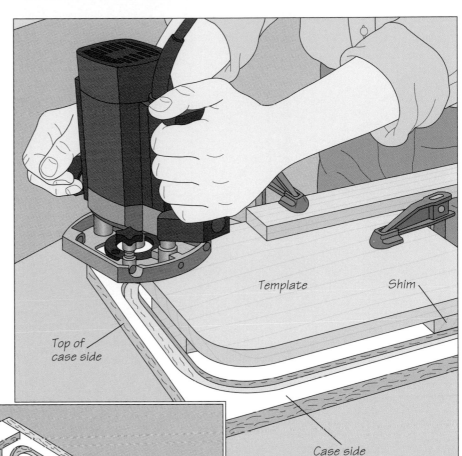

Top of case side

Template

Shim

Case side

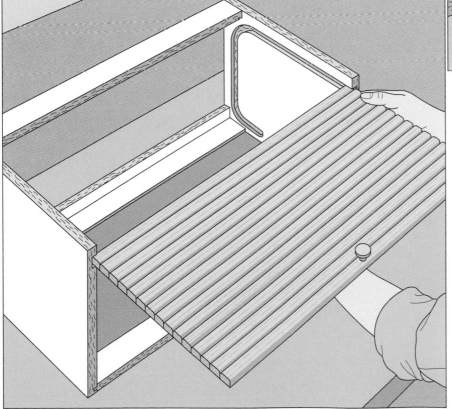

4 Installing the door

Once the sides are prepared you can assemble the case for the appliance bay. Make the width of the case equal to the length of the slats plus the thickness of the sides, less the combined depth of the grooves. (Also add $\frac{1}{16}$ inch to give the door a bit of play.) Note that the appliance bay has no top or bottom; it is designed to fit between the countertop and upper cabinet, and the lack of a bottom panel makes it easier to slide the appliance in and out. To install the tambour door, tilt the case onto its back, then simply slide the door from the bottom *(left)*. The bottom of the door will rest on the counter and its weight will hold it up when opened, therefore no stops or latches are required.

INSTALLING A LAZY SUSAN

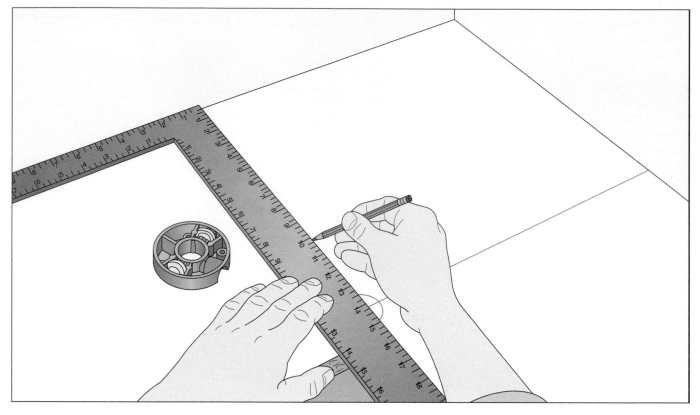

1 Finding the pivot point
A lazy Susan's trays rotate around a central post screwed to the top and bottom of a corner cabinet. To locate the pivot point of the shaft, place one of the trays on the floor of the cabinet and adjust it so its circumference clears the two back panels by about 1 inch. Slide a pencil in the tray's shaft hole and trace a circle. (The manufacturer may provide a positioning template to make this step easier.) Then use a framing square to locate the point in the circle that is the same distance from each back panel *(above)*. This is the pivot point. Transfer these measurements to the top panel—or the nailer if the cabinet has no top.

2 Centering the pivot brackets
Center the lower pivot bracket on the pivot point *(right)*, then screw the hardware in place. Turn the cabinet upside down and repeat to install the upper bracket.

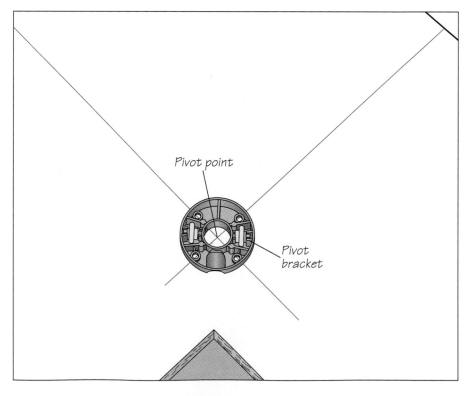

Pivot point

Pivot bracket

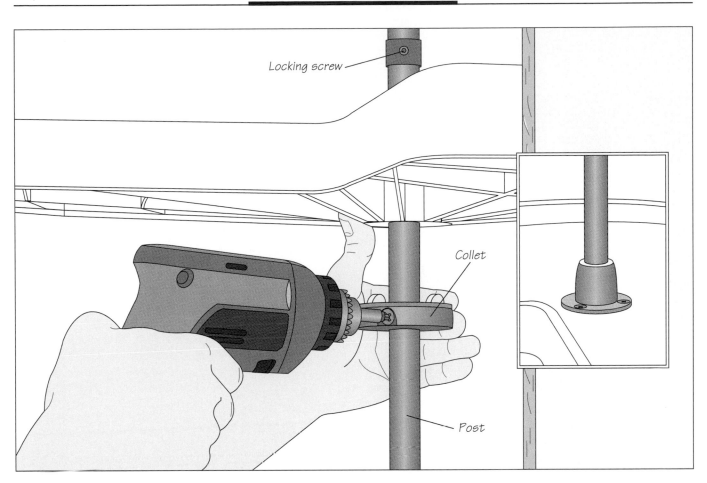

Locking screw

Collet

Post

SHOP TIP

Slide-out shelves
Shelves that slide out of a cabinet not only reduce back strain and time spent rummaging through lower cabinets, they also increase usable storage space. To keep the contents of the shelves from sliding off, glue edging strips cut from ³⁄₄-inch hardwood stock to the shelf sides and ends. Install bottom-mounted shelf slides as you would for a drawer (page 87).

2 Installing the post and trays
For the model of lazy Susan shown, the post consists of two telescoping rods that are extended to fit the cabinet once the trays are slid in place. Slide the lower tray onto the post *(inset)*, followed by the collet and upper tray. Place the post in the bottom pivot bracket, then extend the rod upward so its top fits in the upper pivot bracket. Tighten the locking screw. Next, position the upper tray at the desired height and mark its location on the post. Lift the tray and align the top of the collet with the mark. Tighten the collet in place *(above)*, then lower the upper tray into position.

ASSEMBLING THE CABINETS

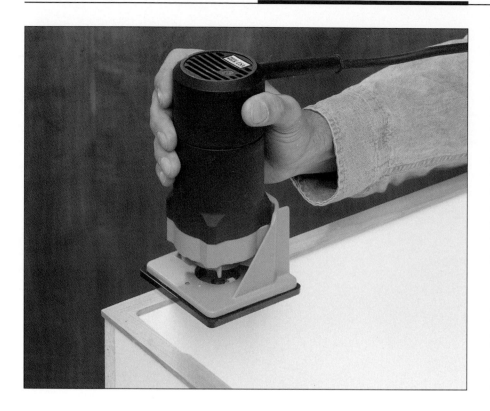

If you have cut the componenents of your cabinets accurately, assembling them will be a straightforward task. While the procedure shown on pages 46-47 is based on biscuit joints, gluing and clamping is identical for most other joinery methods.

If your cabinets do not have sides that extend below their bottom panels, you will need to install legs to support them. Commercial leveler legs *(below)* are quickly bolted in place and allow you to install a level run of cabinets on an uneven floor. They also accommodate a bracket for a clip-on kickplate.

Hiding the edges of melamine or plywood cabinets is essential for a clean, professional look. Here a laminate trimmer cuts solid wood edging flush with the sides of a cabinet. For more on edge treatments, see pages 48-49.

INSTALLING ADJUSTABLE LEGS

1 Drilling holes for the leg bolts

Position the legs on the cabinet bottoms so that when the kickplate is clipped onto the front legs *(page 104)*, it will be inset from the cabinet's front edge by about 4 inches. The legs should also be set in from the sides of the cabinet by the same amount. The simple lipped jig shown at right will help you bore the holes for the leg bolts in exactly the same place on all cabinets. To make the jig, screw two pieces of 1-inch-square stock to one corner of a piece of plywood. Mark a line 4 inches plus the thickness of the kickplate from the inside edge of each lip, then drill a hole in the plywood where the lines intersect. Make the holes for the legs by holding the jig in position and drilling a hole in each corner of the cabinet bottom panel *(right)*.

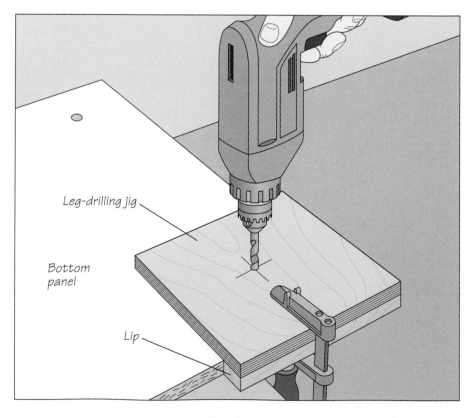

Leg-drilling jig

Bottom panel

Lip

2 Attaching the leg bases

Lay the bottom panel face-down on a work surface. Insert a bolt with a washer through one of the holes you drilled in the previous step, and thread one of the leg bases onto the bolt. Holding the base so that its round surface faces the front of the cabinet *(right)*, tighten the bolt snugly. Then install the other leg bases.

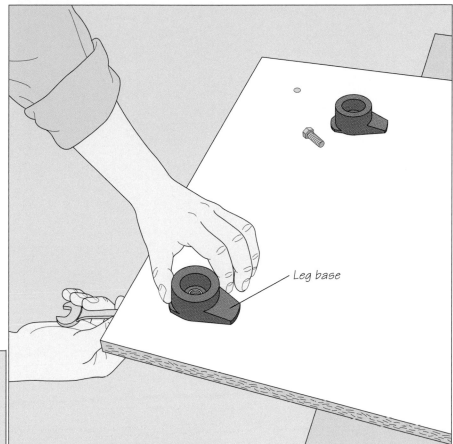

Leg base

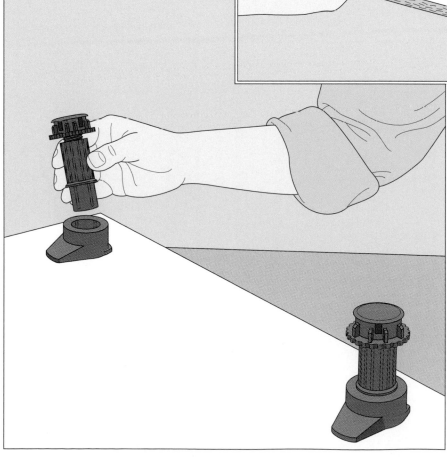

3 Inserting the legs

The final step is to insert the legs in the bases. The type of leveler leg shown at left has matching grooves and ridges. Simply place the leg in the base and push down lightly while turning until it snaps into place. The leg height can then be adjusted when the cabinet is installed *(page 104)*.

GLUING AND CLAMPING THE CABINETS

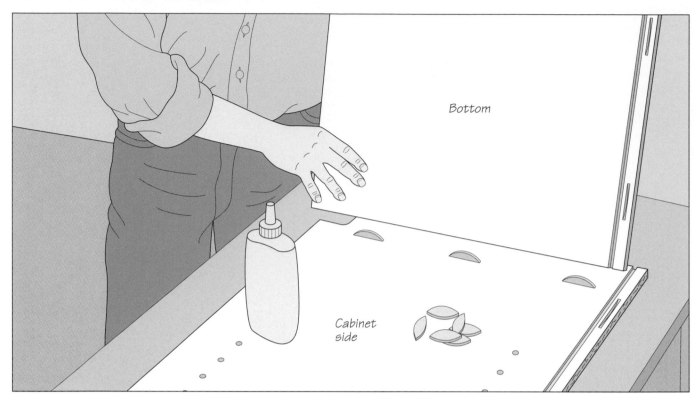

1 Assembling the first corner
Lay one of the cabinet sides face-up on a work surface, insert glue in each biscuit slot, and add the correct-sized biscuits. Apply glue to the exposed biscuits, then fit the cabinet bottom onto the side panel, matching the biscuits and slots.

2 Adding the nailers
Hold the bottom panel in place with a 90° clamp or a combination of handscrews and clamps as shown in the next step. Apply glue in the slots for the rear and countertop nailers and place the biscuits in the slots. Apply glue to the nailers and set them in place. Insert a spacer between the rear nailers to create a gap between the two that will allow you to slide the back into place (*step 4*). Clamp the assembly together (*right*).

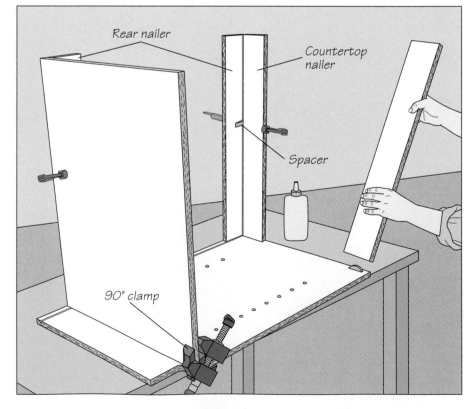

3 Installing the second side

Apply glue to the exposed edges of the bottom panel and the nailers. Insert the biscuits, then set the second side panel atop the assembly *(left)*.

4 Clamping the cabinet

With the cabinet still on its side, slide it so that one edge extends off the work surface. Remove the 90° clamp holding the bottom and install a bar clamp across the front of the cabinet, aligning it with the bottom panel. Repeat this procedure to secure the rest of the case. You will need five bar clamps: two for the case bottom and one each for the two countertop nailers and upper rear nailer. Protect the side panels with wood pads; place a ¼-inch wood chip under the bottom pads to focus some of the pressure midway between the edges of the panel. Make sure all edges are flush and check the cabinet for square before tightening the clamps. Finally, set the assembly on the floor and slide the back panel into position *(right)*.

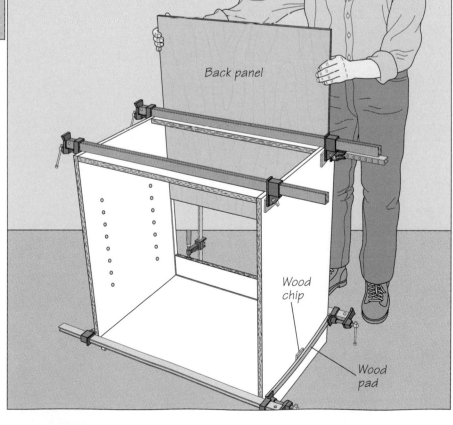

Back panel

Wood chip

Wood pad

SOLID WOOD EDGING

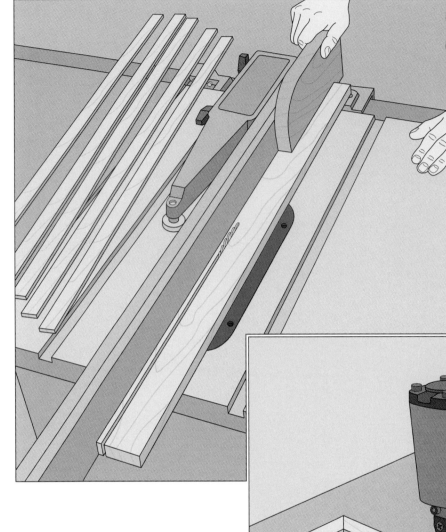

1 Making the edging
Make solid wood edging by ripping it from a piece of stock slightly thicker than your cabinet panels; this will allow you to trim it flush after installation. Plane a length of hardwood stock such as maple or oak to the desired thickness. Set the rip fence on your table saw to cut a ¼-inch-thick strip. Feed the workpiece into the blade *(left)*, keeping light pressure against the fence; finish the cut with a push block. Rip four pieces of edging for each cabinet, cutting them slightly longer than the cabinet.

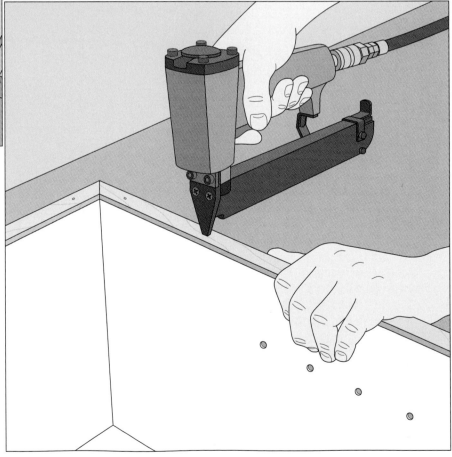

2 Installing the edging
Miter the strips at a 45° angle on each end. Trim the edging to fit as you install it. First cut the edging for the longest sides to the exact height of the cabinet. Spread a thin bead of glue on the mating surfaces, and fasten the edging to the cabinet with finishing nails and a nail gun *(right)* or a hammer. If you are using a hammer, drill pilot holes for the nails to avoid splitting the wood. Cut the top and bottom pieces slightly longer than the width of the cabinet, then trim them until they fit. Glue and nail them in place. Finally, trim the edging flush with the cabinet using a router *(photo, page 44)*.

COMMERCIAL EDGE BANDING

1 Applying commercial edge banding

Commercial edge banding is another method of hiding the edges of melamine; simply choose a color that matches your cabinets. The commercial edge-banding unit shown at right works by feeding the panel along a fence; an adjustable heater melts the banding's adhesive just before it contacts the edge of the panel. Practice on some scrap stock until you find a temperature and feed rate that works well. An inexpensive but more time-consuming alternative is to install commercial edge banding on your cabinets using an iron set on high heat, making sure you do not let the iron rest in one place.

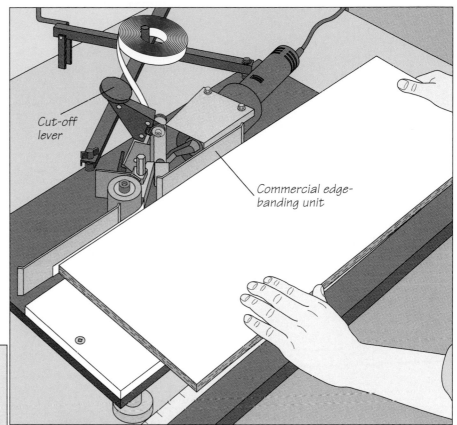

Cut-off lever

Commercial edge-banding unit

Edge trimmer

2 Trimming the edges of the banding

At the ends, push the banding around the corner with the flat side of a chisel to break it cleanly, then cut it off with a downward slice of the chisel. Use an edge trimmer to trim the edges. The model shown features two spring-mounted razor cutters and can fit any panel between $\frac{9}{16}$ and 1 inch thick. Place the trimmer on the edge of the panel at one end and squeeze the two edges together, then pull it slowly and smoothly along the edge *(left)*. You can also use a wide, very sharp chisel for the job. Hold the tool flat to the panel, 45° to the edge, and move along in a single stroke—one for each side of the panel. Finish with either sandpaper or a smooth file for a perfectly flush edge.

FACE FRAMES

A face frame is a solid wood fronting applied to kitchen cabinets. Face frames are not essential; in fact they are noticeably absent on European-style cabinets, whose concealed, micro-adjustable hinges make it possible to install doors that seamlessly cover the entire cabinet front. However, face frames can add a traditional look to a European kitchen.

When laying out a face frame, remember to add an extra ½ inch to any stile positioned next to a wall; this will allow you to scribe and trim the stile if the wall is out-of-plumb. If the cabinet has drawers, you will also require dividers between them. If your cabinets feature fully recessed doors and drawers, cock-beading *(page 53)* can add a subtle, decorative touch.

Face frames can be joined in a number of ways, including pocket holes, biscuits, and dowels. Here, a commercial pocket hole cutter bores a hole in a face frame rail. Pocket holes can also be used to attach the face frame to the cabinet; be sure to cut the holes in the case sides and rails before assembling them.

ANATOMY OF A FACE FRAME

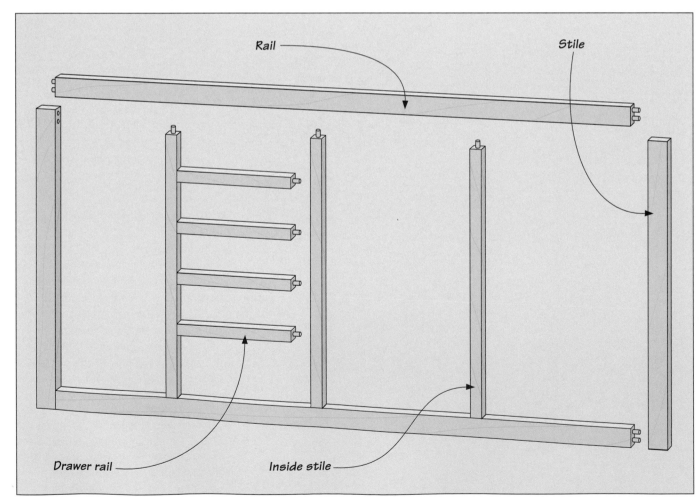

Rail

Stile

Drawer rail

Inside stile

JOINING FACE FRAMES WITH DOWELS

1 Drilling holes

Use a doweling jig to drill holes for dowels in the face frame members. The model shown at right not only aligns the holes in both rails and stiles, but also holds the bit exactly perpendicular to the wood surface. Follow the manufacturer's instructions to set up the jig for the thickness of the face frame stock, then adjust the jig to drill two holes about ½ inch in from either end of one of the stiles. Insert the bushing that matches the dowel diameter into the bushing carrier of the jig, and attach a collet to the drill bit and adjust it to bore a hole 1/16 inch deeper than half the length of the dowels. (Allow for the thickness of the jig and bushing when making this measurement.) Clamp a stile in your workbench and place the jig on the stile, aligning it with one end of the workpiece. Set the bushing carrier in the appropriate hole in the doweling jig. Holding the jig steady, drill the hole. Repeat to drill the second hole, then bore the holes at the opposite end of the stile, in both ends of all rails *(right)*, and in any inside stiles that also require dowel holes.

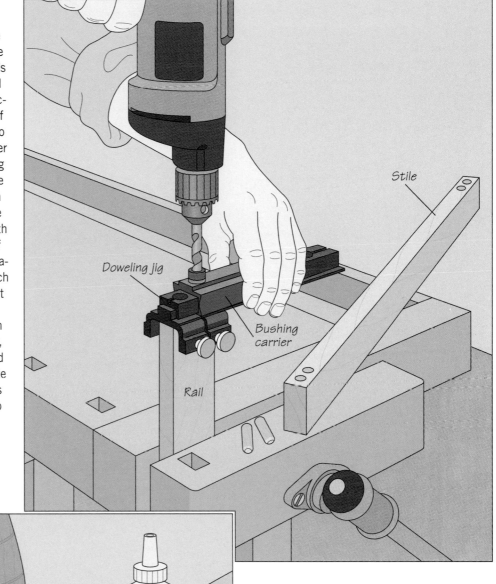

Stile

Doweling jig

Bushing carrier

Rail

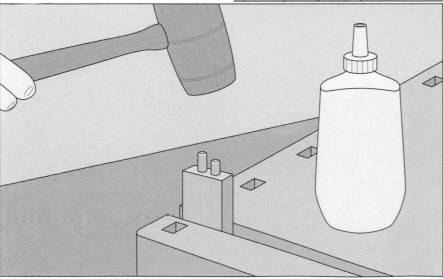

2 Inserting the dowels

Insert dowels in the drawer rails and inside stiles first, then in the outer stiles. To insert the dowels, clamp the appropriate frame member to your bench, spread glue on one end of the dowel, then tap it home with a mallet *(left)*. Assemble the frame *(page 53)*.

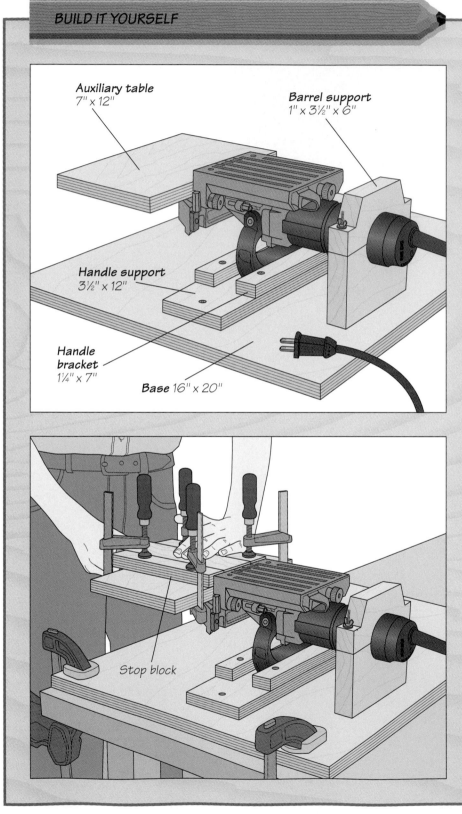

Auxiliary table
7" x 12"

Barrel support
1" x 3½" x 6"

Handle support
3½" x 12"

Handle
bracket
1¼" x 7"

Base 16" x 20"

Stop block

PLATE JOINER STAND

To reduce the setup time needed to cut slots for biscuit-jointed face frames, mount your plate joiner in a shop-made stand like the one shown at left. Build the jig from ¾-inch plywood, except for the barrel support, which should be solid wood. Refer to the illustration for suggested dimensions.

Screw the handle support to the base, then attach the handle brackets, spacing them to fit your tool. With the plate joiner resting upside down on the handle support, butt the barrel support against the motor housing and trace the outline of the barrel on the stock. Cut or bore a hole for the barrel, then saw the support in two across its width, through the center of the hole. Screw the bottom part to the base and fit the other half on top. Bore holes for hanger bolts through the top on each side of the opening, then drive the hanger bolts into the bottom of the support. For quick installation and removal of the tool, use wing nuts to hold the two halves together.

Screw the auxiliary table to the fixed-angle fence of the joiner. (It may be necessary to drill holes in the fence to accept the screws.)

To use the stand, secure the joiner in it, then clamp the base to a work surface. Set the fence at the correct height and, for repeat cuts, clamp stop blocks to the auxiliary table to center the workpiece on the cutter wheel. To cut a slot, put the workpiece flat on the table and butted against the joiner's faceplate, then turn on the tool and push the stock and the table toward the cutter (left, below).

ASSEMBLING THE FACE FRAME

Clamping up the frame

Assemble the frame working from the middle outward, gluing up any drawer rails and inside stiles first. In the frame shown at right, start by gluing the inside stile to the two face frame rails. Apply glue to the exposed dowels then push the rails into place. Tighten the assembly with a bar clamp. Next, spread some glue on the dowels in the rails and install the other stiles; tighten them in place with two more bar clamps. Check the assembly for square by measuring across the two diagonals *(right)*. They should be equal. If not, place a bar clamp across the longer diagonal and tighten it until the frame is square.

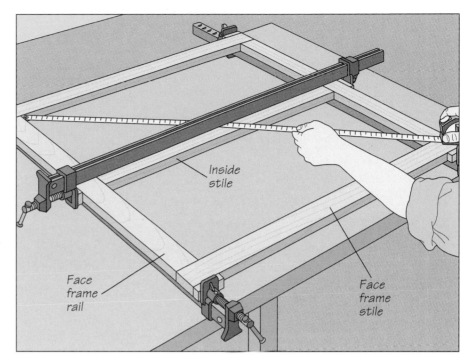

Inside stile

Face frame rail

Face frame stile

INSTALLING COCKBEADING

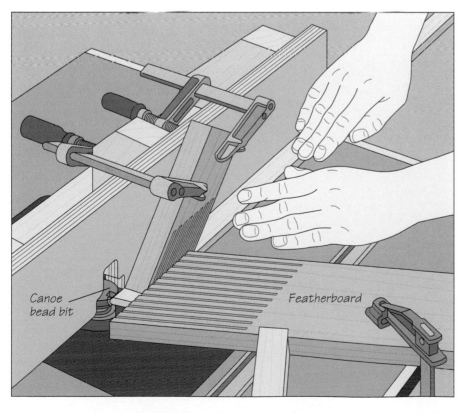

Canoe bead bit

Featherboard

1 Making cockbeading

Make cockbeading as you made solid wood edging *(page 48)*, ripping ¼ inch-thick strips from a piece of hardwood stock ¼ inch thicker than the thickness of the face frame. To round over the outside edge of the cockbeading, install a ¼-inch canoe bead bit in a router and install the tool in a table. Raise the height of the bit so it is centered on the stock, and adjust the position of the fence to just behind the cutter. Attach a featherboard to the table to hold the stock against the fence, and clamp two more featherboards to the fence on either side of the bit to prevent the stock from lifting up. (In the illustration, the front featherboard has been removed for clarity.) With the workpiece lying flat on the table, feed it into the bit *(left)*, finishing the cut with a push stick. Rip the cockbeading to width and then cut it to length, mitering the ends at 45°.

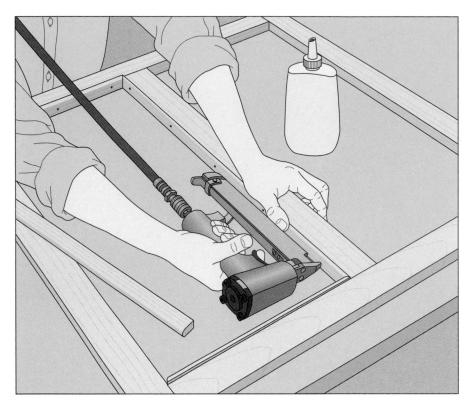

2 **Installing the cockbeading**
Dry fit the cockbeading strips; pare any ill-fitting joints with a chisel. Lay the frame on a flat surface. Spread some glue on the outside face of a strip of cockbeading and position it on the frame, aligning the back edges of the two. Drive in finishing nails with a hammer or an air nailer *(left)*.

INSTALLING THE FACE FRAME

Attaching the face frame to the casework
Apply some glue to the edges of the cabinet. Place the face frame in position and align it with the top, bottom, and sides of the cabinet. In the illustration at right, the right side of the frame overhangs the cabinet; this is to allow the stile of the face frame to be trimmed to fit the profile of the wall *(page 104)*. Fasten the face frame in place with a finishing nail every 4-6 inches.

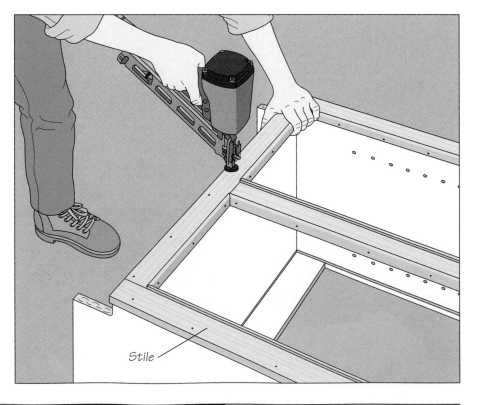

Stile

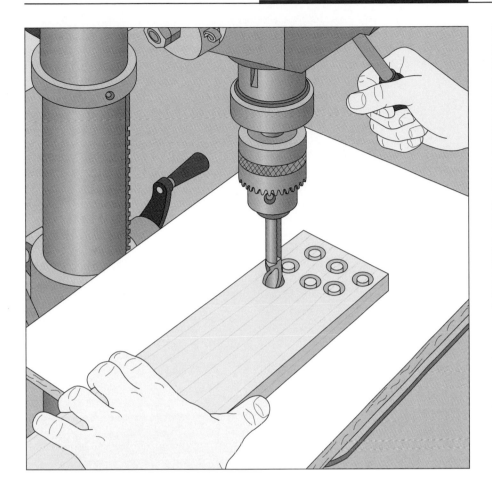

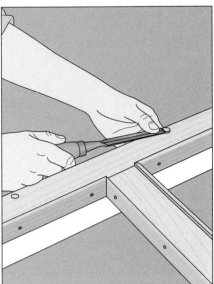

Using screws and wood plugs

If you are installing your face frames with screws, counterbore the fasteners and cover their heads with wood plugs. Position the frame in place as you would for face-nailing *(page 54)*, drill and counterbore screw holes, then drive the screws in place. To make the plugs, install a plug cutter the same diameter as the counterbored holes in your drill press. Choosing some wood that matches the frame stock for grain and color, bore as many plugs as you need in the stock *(above, left)*. Pry the plugs free with a screwdriver or narrow chisel. (See the Shop Tip at left for an alternate procedure.) To install the plugs, apply glue in the hole, then tap the plug in place. Trim the excess with a chisel. Holding the chisel bevel-side up on the frame, remove the waste in fine shavings *(above, right)* until the plug is perfectly flush. This will produce a much cleaner surface than if the plug were sanded flush.

SHOP TIP

Making wood plugs

Save time making wood plugs by using a piece of tape to remove them from their holes. Use a plug cutter on the drill press to bore a row of plugs to the depth you require. Cover the row with a strip of masking tape, then rip the plugs to length on the band saw. Simply peel off the tape to remove the row of plugs.

DOORS

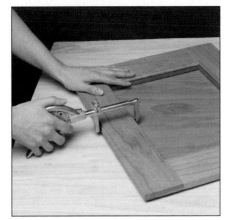

A brad driver secures a strip of molding to the frame of a kitchen cabinet door, sandwiching a central pane of glass between the molding and a rabbet cut into the inside edge of the frame. For more on building glass doors, see page 69.

Cabinet doors are arguably the most important single decorative feature of a kitchen. They are the first item to greet the eye and, because they are usually so numerous, can also be the most impressive. The style, finish, and construction deserve careful attention.

Once, cabinetmakers were concerned primarily with building simple, sturdy doors that would stand up to the punishment meted out to them in daily use. Form certainly followed function by a wide margin; kitchen cabinets, and especially their doors, were the most utilitarian of furniture. But gone are the days of one-style-fits-all kitchens. Today, homeowners carefully consider the period and style of their dwellings before determining the decor of their kitchens. Some of the possibilities are shown in the Layout And Design chapter *(page 16)*.

Once the basic choice is made, door style can be arrived at. Perhaps it is a basic board-and-batten door *(page 60)* for a country cottage. An Arts and Crafts bungalow might demand finer work, with doors featuring glass panes set in glazing bars *(page 70)*. Most homeowners will probably prefer traditional frame-and-panel doors *(page 62)*. But even here there are variations, such as arched panel *(page 67)*, veneered panel *(page 68)*, and glass panel doors *(page 69)*. This chapter introduces five door styles and the steps to building each, so you can produce doors that will lend character to your kitchen.

Considerations of style should not cloud the need for durability. Kitchen doors work hard and, since wood is prone to swelling and warping, solid doors such as board-and-batten doors should only be installed on small cabinets. Frame-and-panel, veneered-panel, and glass doors are better able to accommodate wood movement caused by fluctuations in heat and humidity. Also, different doors require different degrees of precision when building them. A flush-mounted door, for example, is cut to close tolerances; an error as slight as $\frac{1}{16}$ inch can spoil the look of an otherwise finely executed cabinet. Overlay doors, on the other hand, do not require the same precision as they exceed the size of their openings.

Advances in the manufacturing of door hardware, particularly hinges, have greatly improved both the appearance of cabinet doors and the ease of mounting them *(page 73)*. Classic or antique-style doors may still be hung from such decorative and attractive fasteners as surface-mounted hinges that come in polished iron or brass finishes. Other hinge options include the simple but efficient butt hinge *(page 76)* for flush-mounted doors, and the piano hinge for corner cabinet doors. European-style cup hinges *(page 74)* have virtually become the standard hardware for melamine kitchen cabinets. Not only are these versatile hinges fully concealed; they are also simple to install and easily adjustable.

The versatile European cup hinge can be used to hang a variety of kitchen cabinet doors. In the photo at left, a full overlay frame-and-panel door is being mounted on a face frame cabinet. The door can be adjusted or removed with ease.

A GALLERY OF CABINET DOOR DESIGNS

Of the four door types shown below and on the following page, all but the board-and-batten door are built using frame-and-panel techniques. The board-and-batten door *(page 60)* is a solid panel door featuring a series of planks with rabbeted edges held together by battens screwed across the back of the door. Frame-and-panel doors *(page 62)* feature a panel that floats within a frame composed of rails and stiles assembled with mortise-and-tenon or cope-and-stick joints. The floating panel in the center of the door can be raised or shaped for decorative effect. The rails and stiles have an integrated molding

cut into them; for added embellishment you can also cut an arch or curve into the upper rail and panel.

Veneered-panel doors *(page 68)* feature a panel made from veneered sheet stock that is glued to the frame. To conceal the plate joints between the panel and the frame, rabbets are cut into the inside edges of the frame at the back. Glass-panel doors *(page 69)* are essentially a frame-and-panel door with a pane of glass replacing a floating panel. The piece of glass sits in rabbets cut along the edges of the frame. It is held in place by strips of molding. A variation of the glass panel

door features glazing bars that hold smaller panes in place *(page 70)*. Joined by mitered half-laps, the glazing bars have rabbets cut along their back edges to accommodate the glass and glass-stop molding.

Although a door is always made to fit its cabinet, it does not always have to be sized exactly to fit its opening, as shown in the illustration on the opposite page. Flush-mounted and full-recess doors can be time-consuming to construct because of the fine tolerances required to fit and hang them properly. They are particularly unsuitable for board-and-batten doors, as these doors tend to

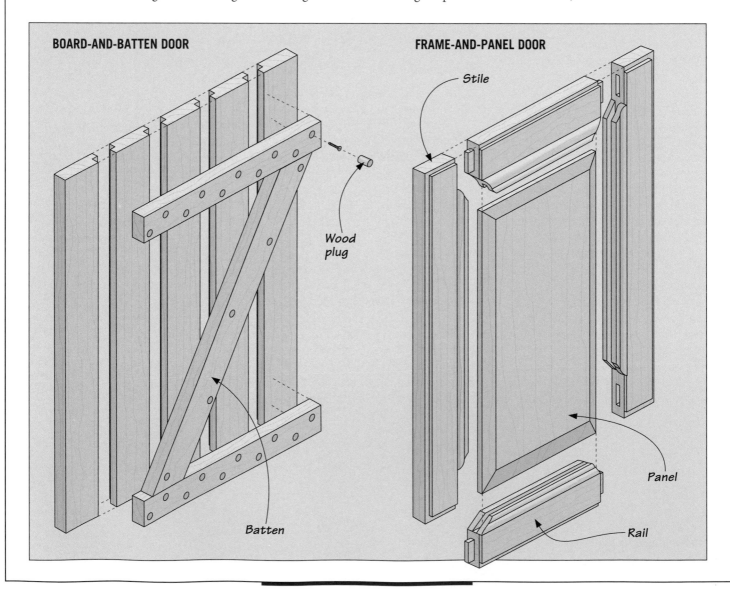

BOARD-AND-BATTEN DOOR

Wood plug

Batten

FRAME-AND-PANEL DOOR

Stile

Panel

Rail

expand and contract with changes in humidity. Full-overlay or lip-rabbeted doors are easier to make. A full-overlay door covers the entire width of the cabinet, while a lip-rabbeted door has rabbets cut around its outside edges at the back so that only a part of its thickness is exposed.

One of the most commonly used doors is the one typically used for European-style cabinets—a piece of laminated particleboard such as melamine simply cut to size. While inexpensive and easier to maintain, melamine doors need edge banding (pages 48-49) to conceal their non-laminated edges.

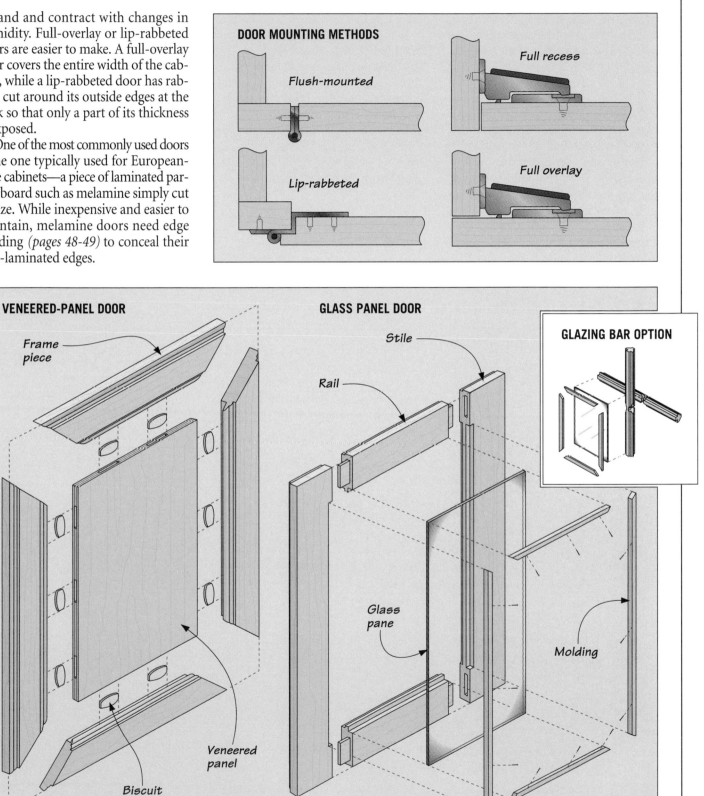

DOOR MOUNTING METHODS

Flush-mounted

Full recess

Lip-rabbeted

Full overlay

VENEERED-PANEL DOOR

Frame piece

Veneered panel

Biscuit

GLASS PANEL DOOR

Stile

Rail

Glass pane

Molding

GLAZING BAR OPTION

BOARD-AND-BATTEN DOORS

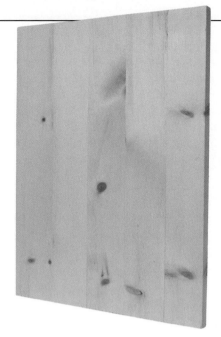

Like their early colonial counterparts, modern cabinetmakers seeking a rustic or "country" look often turn to board-and-batten doors. These simple but sturdy doors consist of rabbeted planks held together by strips or battens of wood fastened across their backs. The most common of these features battens screwed to the back of the door in the form of a Z; the diagonal batten connecting the two horizontal battens at the top and bottom acts as a brace to strengthen the door and prevent sagging.

Because they are solid panel doors and will swell and shrink with changes in humidity, board-and-batten doors are often mounted on smaller cabinets as overlay doors. In some cases, the battens can interfere with interior shelving. One solution is to recess the battens in dadoes cut into the back of the doors. Another more elaborate method of bracing a board-and-batten door is to rout a sliding dovetail across the back of the boards. Rout a matching dovetail slide in the battens, and secure them in place with a single screw in the center of the door.

Combining rustic strength and charm, board-and-batten doors are ideal for small cupboards in a country kitchen.

JOINTS USED IN BOARD-AND-BATTEN DOORS

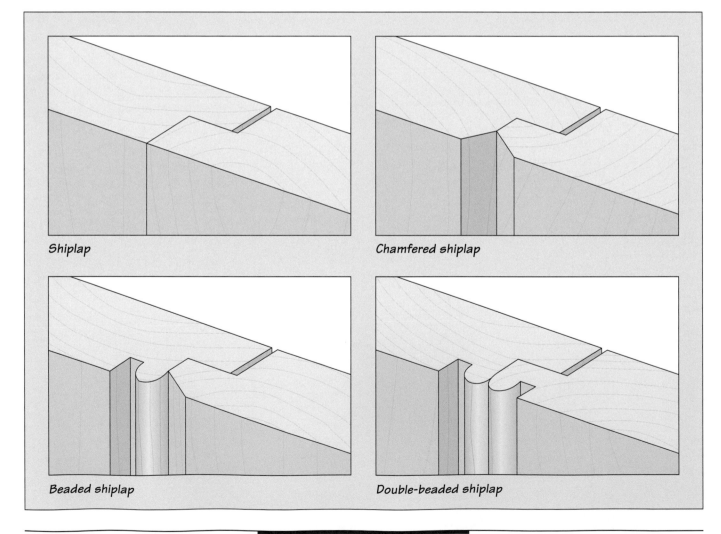

Shiplap

Chamfered shiplap

Beaded shiplap

Double-beaded shiplap

MAKING A BOARD-AND-BATTEN DOOR

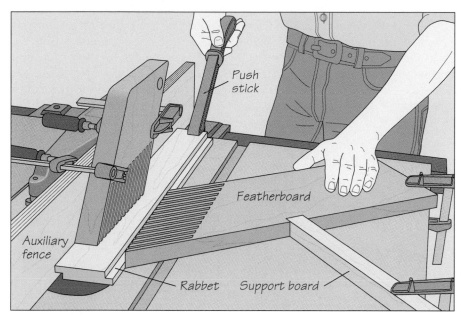

1 Cutting the rabbets

Install a dado head half as wide as the stock thickness on your table saw. Attach an auxiliary wood fence and raise the blades to cut a notch in it, then set the cutting height—again one-half the thickness of the boards. To secure the workpiece, clamp two featherboards and a support board to the table as shown. Using a push stick, feed the stock into the blades, then flip the board over and repeat the cut along the other edge *(left)*. To allow for wood movement, create a slight expansion gap between the boards at the back of the door by running one edge of each board across the jointer.

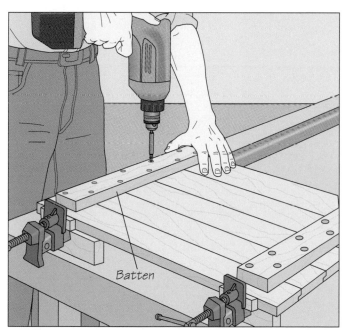

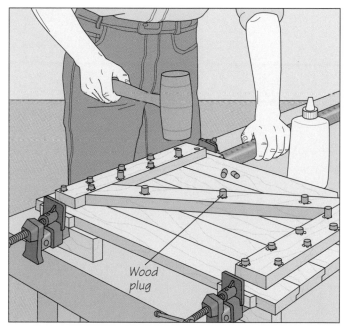

2 Assembling the door

Clamp the door together and place it inside-face up on a work surface. Then cut two battens slightly shorter than the width of the door and narrower than the door boards. Position the two pieces of wood across the top and bottom of the assembly as shown. Then fit an electric drill with a combination bit and counterbore holes for screws and wood plugs at 2-inch intervals along the battens, alternating between the top and bottom of each board. Make clearance holes except in the places where the screw will join the batten to an outside door board. Then, holding the batten square to the edge of the door, drive in each screw *(above, left)*. Cut a third batten to fit diagonally between the two already in place and screw it into position. To conceal the screws, apply a dab of glue to their heads, then insert plugs in the holes. Tap the plugs in place with a wooden mallet *(above, right)*, then use a chisel to trim the projecting stubs flush with the door surface.

FRAME-AND-PANEL DOORS

Pleasing to the eye and structurally sound, the frame-and-panel door is the most enduring and popular of all cabinet door designs. Because its panel floats in a rigid frame of rails and stiles, a frame-and-panel door withstands the swelling and shrinking of wood brought on by changes in humidity better than any other solid-wood door. The flexibility of its design allows for a wide variety of attractive options, such as veneered panels *(page 68)*, glass doors *(page 69)*, and glazing bars *(page 70)*. The top rail of the frame can even be arched to soften the rectangular lines of the doors and add a touch of elegance *(page 67)*.

The frame derives its considerable strength from the joinery methods used in its construction. This section covers building a frame-and-panel door using mortise-and-tenon joinery with integrated molding *(page 63)* and cope-and-stick joints *(page 66)*. Before starting to build a frame-and-panel door, however, take care to size the stock properly. Make the stiles equal to the height of the door opening; the rails should be as long as the width of the door plus the two tenons at either end—typically about ¾ inch—minus the width of the stiles.

Depending on the desired appearance of a frame-and-panel door, the panel's inside edges can be molded to fit in the grooves of the frame or beveled on four sides to "raise" the center of the panel. In the photo at left, a panel is being raised with an ogee panel-raising bit on a router table.

RAISED PANEL STYLES

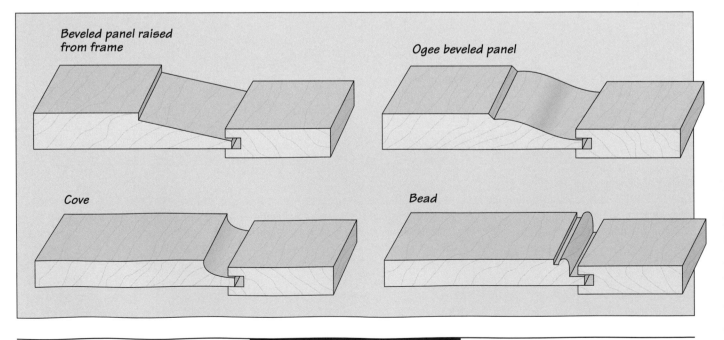

Beveled panel raised from frame

Ogee beveled panel

Cove

Bead

MAKING A FRAME-AND-PANEL DOOR

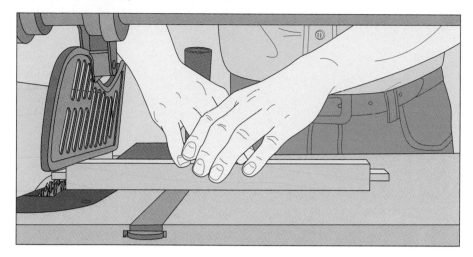

1 Cutting the tenon cheeks
Install a dado head slightly wider than the tenon length on your table saw. Attach and notch an auxiliary fence, then set the width of cut equal to the length of the tenon to saw the tenon cheeks; adjust the cutting height to about one-third the thickness of the stock. Butting the rail against the fence and the miter gauge, feed the stock face down into the blades. Turn the rail over and repeat the cut on the other side of the tenon. Then repeat the process at the opposite end of the rail *(left)* and with the second rail.

2 Cutting the tenon shoulders
To cut the tenon shoulders, set the height of the dado head at about ½ inch. Standing the rail on edge flush against the fence and miter gauge, feed the workpiece into the blades. Turn the rail over and repeat on the other side of the tenon. Cut the tenon shoulders at the opposite end of the rail the same way *(right)*. Repeat the process with the second rail. To add integrated molding, fit a router with the appropriate bit, mount the tool in a router table and cut along the inside edges of the rails and stiles.

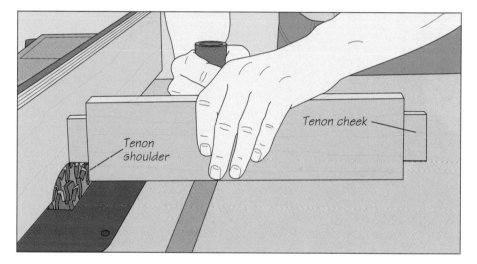

Tenon shoulder

Tenon cheek

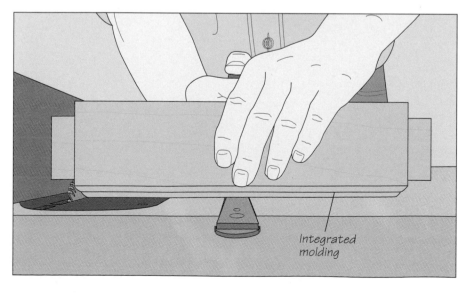

Integrated molding

3 Preparing the rails for glue up
Remove the auxiliary fence and dado head. Install a combination blade and adjust its angle to 45°. To set the width of cut, mark a line on the molded edge of a rail the same distance from the tenon shoulder as the molding width. Align the mark with the blade where it exits the table opening, then butt the fence against the rail. Adjust the blade height until one tooth protrudes just beyond the tenon shoulder. To make the cuts, butt the rail against the fence and hold it flush against the miter gauge to feed it molded-edge down into the blade. Repeat to cut the other end of the rail *(left)* and both ends of the second rail.

4 Preparing the stiles

Mark a line on the molded edge of each stile the width of a rail away from the end of the board. With the table saw blade angled at 45°, align the cutting edge with the mark and cut into the molded edge; adjust the cutting height so the cut finishes at the point where the molding ends and the face of the stile begins. Next, slice off the strip of molding between the 45° cut and the end of the stile with a band saw *(right)*.

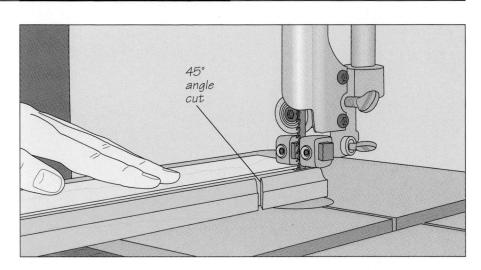

5 Smoothing the cut edge

On the table saw, adjust the rip fence so the blade lines up with the beginning of the cut you made in step 1 when the stile is butted against the fence. Hold the stile flush against the miter gauge. Slide the stock back and forth along the miter gauge to smooth the cut edge *(left)*.

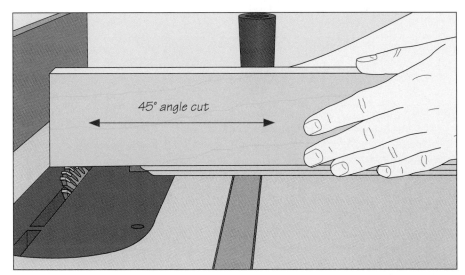

6 Cutting the mortises

Cut the mortises in the stiles on a drill press using a commercial mortising attachment. Align a rail with each stile and mark the outline of the mortises. Install a mortising attachment on your drill press and clamp the stile to the fence, centering the mortise outline under the chisel and bit. Set the drilling depth slightly deeper than the tenon length, then make a cut at each end of the mortise before boring out the waste in between *(right)*.

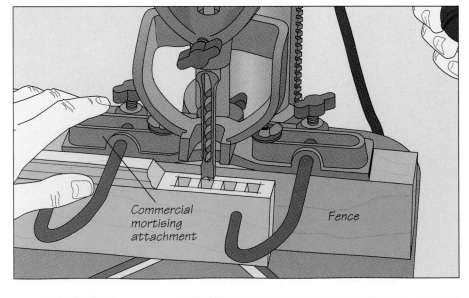

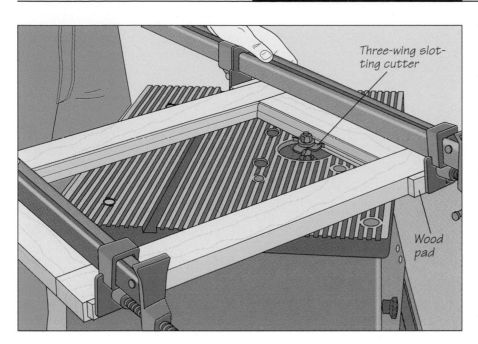

Three-wing slotting cutter

Wood pad

7 Cutting grooves for the panel

Assemble the rails and stiles. Then, protecting the stock with wood pads, use two bar clamps to hold the frame together securely. Fit a router with a ¼-inch three-wing slotting cutter and mount the tool in a router table. Remove the fence and set the frame on the table. Adjust the cutter height to place the groove midway between the bottom of the frame and the edge of the molding. Gripping the bar clamps firmly, butt the inside edge of the frame against the bit near one corner, then rotate it against the direction of bit rotation to cut the groove along the rails and stiles *(left)*. Keep the frame flat on the table as you feed it into the bit. Raise a panel to fit the frame *(photo, page 62)*, then disassemble the frame.

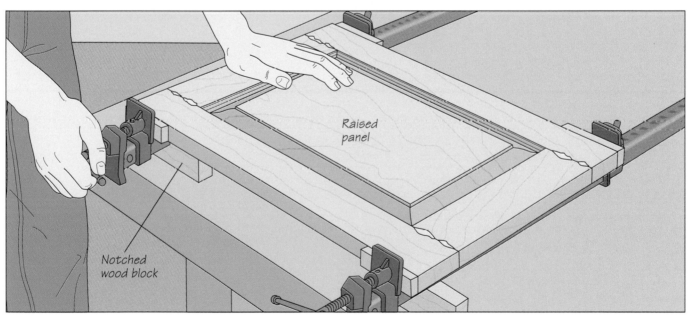

Raised panel

Notched wood block

8 Gluing up the door

Glue up a panel from ¾-inch-thick solid stock and cut it to size; adding ¼ inch to each side to allow the panel to fit the groove in the frame. Then rout the edges of the panel to produce the raised center, as shown in the photo on page 62. Make successive passes until the edge of the panel fits into the groove in the frame. To reduce tearout, rout the top and bottom edges before routing the sides. Squeeze some glue into the mortises in the stiles and on the tenon cheeks and shoulders at the ends of the rails; also apply some adhesive on the contacting surfaces of the miter cuts in the rails and stiles. Do not add any glue to the panel grooves. Then, assemble the door and set on two bar clamps on a work surface, aligning the rails with the bars of the clamps. To keep the clamps from falling over, prop each one on a notched wood block. Protecting the frame with wood pads, tighten the clamps just enough to fully close the joints *(above)*, then use a square to check whether the corners of the door are at right angles. Finish tightening the clamps until the glue squeezes out of the joints, checking occasionally that the corners remain square. Once the glue has dried, use a cabinet scraper to remove any remaining adhesive.

COPE-AND-STICK JOINERY

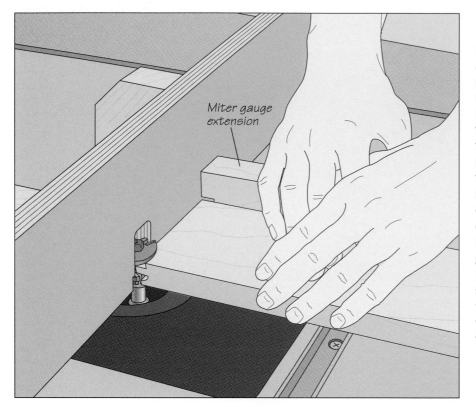

Miter gauge extension

1 Cutting tongues in the rails
The cope-and-stick joint provides a method of joining stiles and rails in frame-and-panel construction. Tongues in the rails mesh with grooves in the stiles; the router bit that cuts the grooves for the panel also carves a decorative molding in the inside edges of the frame. To cut the tongues, install a piloted coping bit—the rail cutter—in your router and mount the tool in a table. Butt the end of a rail against the bit and adjust the depth of cut so that the top of the uppermost cutter is slightly above the workpiece. Position the fence parallel to the miter gauge slot in line with the edge of the bit pilot. Fit the miter gauge with an extension and lay the outside face of the stock flat on the table; keep the ends of the workpiece and extension butted against the fence throughout each cut *(left)*.

2 Cutting the grooves
Unplug the router and replace the coping bit with a piloted sticking bit—also known as a stile cutter. To set the cutting depth, butt the end of a completed rail against the stile cutter; adjust the height of the bit until one of its cutters is level with the rail tongue *(inset)*. Align the fence with the edge of the pilot bearing. Use two featherboards to secure the workpiece during the cut: Clamp one to the router table opposite the bit and secure the other on the infeed side of the fence. Make each cut with the stock outside-face down, pressing the inside edge of the workpiece against the fence *(right)*. Use a push stick to complete the pass. Repeat on the inside edges of all rails and stiles.

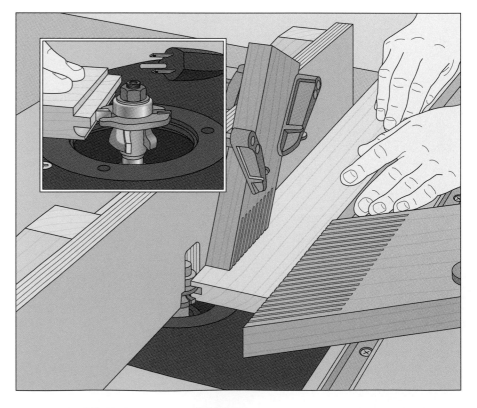

RAISING AN ARCHED PANEL

1 Raising the arch
Bandsaw the panel to size, adding ¼ inch on each side to allow the panel to fit the groove in the frame. Install a panel-raising bit in your router and mount the tool in a table, setting it for a shallow cut. Clamp a free-standing bit guard to the table, and a guide extending from the infeed end of the table to the bit's pilot bearing. (Do not use a fence for this operation, as you will need to pivot the panel beyond the bit.) Using the guide as a pivot point *(right)*, pivot one end of the arch into the bit and start routing the arch, keeping the panel flush with the pilot bearing throughout the cut. Make several passes on the arch, raising the bit ⅛ inch at a time until the panel fits the groove in the frame.

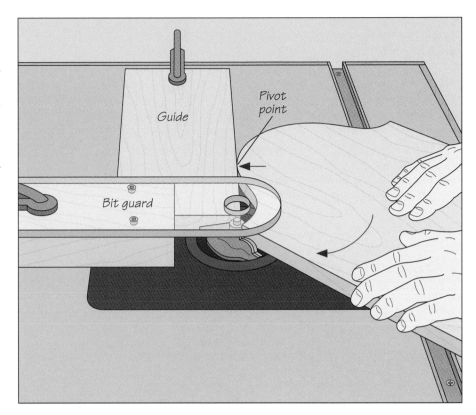

Guide

Pivot point

Bit guard

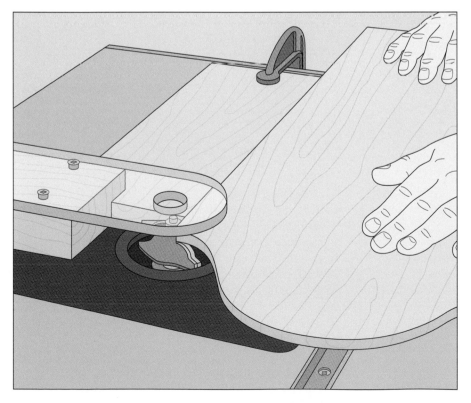

2 Raising the sides
To raise the sides and end of the panel, use the same setup or remove the guide and bit guard and install a fence on your router table. Lower the bit to a shallow cutting depth. Then, holding the panel flat on the table, feed it into the bit with your right hand and press it flat against the guide with your left *(left)*. Repeat for the other side and the end of the panel. Make as many passes as necessary for the panel to fit in the grooves in the frame, raising the bit ⅛ inch at a time and testing between passes. Then glue up the door as you would a regular frame-and-panel assembly *(page 65, step 8)*.

VEENERED-PANEL DOOR

1 Preparing the frame pieces

Rip the four frame pieces to width, then crosscut them slightly longer than their finished length. Fit a router with a decorative molding bit, install the tool in a router table, and rout the outside edge of each frame piece. Next, cut a rabbet in the back face of each of frame piece. Set the cutting height to equal the thickness of the panel; the width should be one-half the stock thickness. Clamp featherboards to the saw table to support the workpiece. Insert a shim between the vertical featherboard and the fence to keep the pressure off the rabbeted part of the stock. Feed the workpiece face up into the dado head *(right)*. Cut the frame pieces to size, making 45° miter cuts at each end. Dry-assemble the frame, then cut the panel to fit it. Mark the panel edges and their mating frame pieces to help you correctly assemble the door at the time of glue up.

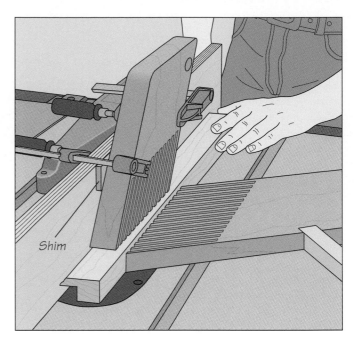

Shim

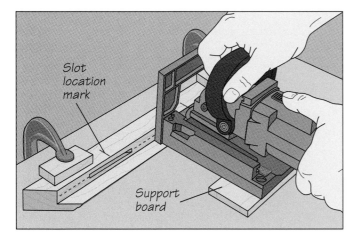

Slot location mark

Support board

2 Cutting biscuit slots in the frames

Cut the panel to size and mark a line across the panel and frame pieces about 4 inches from each edge and at 6-inch intervals in between. Disassemble the door and clamp one frame piece to a work surface, protecting the stock with wood pads. Set the proper depth of a cut on a plate joiner, then set the tool's base plate on the bottom of the rabbet in the frame piece. Set the cutting height so the slots will be made in the middle of the rabbeted portion of the frame, as shown by the red dotted line in the illustration. With a support board under the joiner to keep it level, align the guideline on the tool with a slot location mark. Holding the joiner with both hands, cut a groove at each mark *(above)*. Repeat for the other frame pieces, then cut the mating slots in the panel the same way.

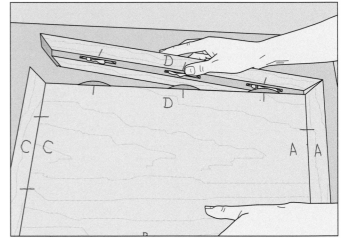

3 Assembling the door

Once all the slots have been cut, glue up the door. Set the frame pieces and the panel face-down on a clean work surface and squeeze glue into each slot, inserting biscuits as you go. To prevent the biscuits from expanding before everything is put together, assemble the doors as quickly as possible, fitting the frame pieces to the panel *(above)*. Set the door on two bar clamps on a work surface. With wood pads protecting the frame, tighten the clamps just enough to close the joints. Install two more clamps, across the top of the door, placing them perpendicular to the first two. Finish tightening until glue squeezes out of the joints. Once the adhesive has dried, remove any excess with a cabinet scraper.

GLASS-PANEL DOOR

1 Cutting a rabbet around the inside of a door frame

Make and glue up a frame as you would for a frame-and-panel door *(page 63)*. Using a wood pad for protection, clamp the frame to a work surface. Then install a ⅜-inch rabbeting bit in a router and set the depth of cut to the combined depth of the molding and the pane of glass you intend to install in the frame. Hold the tool firmly with both hands while resting the baseplate on the frame near one corner, then turn on the router and guide the bit into the inside edge of the door. Move the router clockwise along the edges *(right)* until the cut is completed. Square the corners with a wooden mallet and a wood chisel *(below)*. Make the cuts against the grain first to avoid splitting the frame.

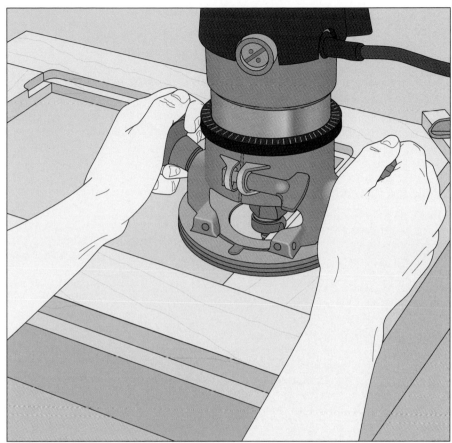

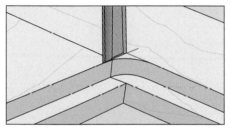

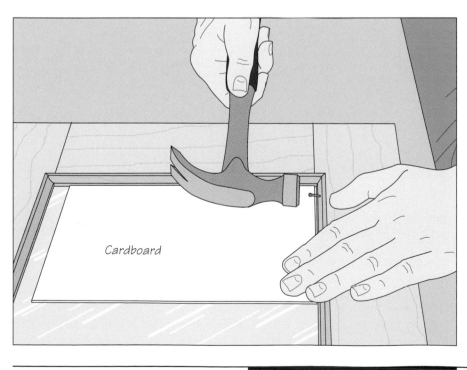

Cardboard

2 Fitting the glass

To hold the glass in the frame, make glass-stop molding by routing a decorative edge in either side of a long piece of solid stock. Rip the molding to width, then miter four pieces to fit the frame. Set the frame and the glass on a work surface, then place the molding in position. Bore a pilot hole every 2 inches using an electric drill fitted with a small finishing nail with the head snipped off. Drive the brads in place using either a hammer or a brad driver *(photo, page 57)*. When using a hammer, hold the molding flush against the frame of the door; slide the hammer along the surface of a piece of cardboard to avoid breaking the glass *(left)*.

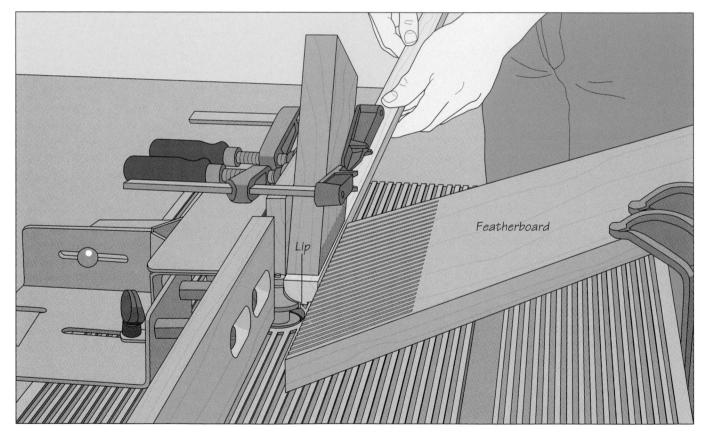

If you prefer the look of smaller panes of glass rather than one larger single pane in your door you can choose to make glazing bars. The molded strips are joined with mitered half-laps. Rabbets are cut along the back edges of the bars to accommodate panes of glass and glass-stop molding. The ends of the bars can be joined to the outer rails and stiles with dowels or cope-and-stick joints.

MAKING A GLAZING BAR DOOR

1 Molding the glazing bars

The joint is made in three stages: Start by cutting the proper profile in the glazing bars, as shown above; next, cut rabbets into the opposite sides of the bars to hold the glass and molding strips *(step 2)*; finally, produce the mitered half-lap *(steps 3 to 5)*. For the first stage, install a piloted roundover bit in a router, mount the tool in a table, and align the fence with the bit's pilot bearing. The stock should be wide enough so that making a pass on each side of the bar will leave a ¼-inch-wide lip between the cuts. Support the workpiece during the operation with three featherboards: Clamp one to the table opposite the bit and two to the fence on each side of the cutter. (In the illustration, the featherboard on the outfeed side of the fence has been removed for clarity). Feed the bar into the bit until your fingers approach the cutter, then use the next piece as a push stick or move to the other side of the table and pull the workpiece through the cut. Repeat the pass on the other side of the bar *(above)*. Prepare an extra bar to help set up the cut in step 3.

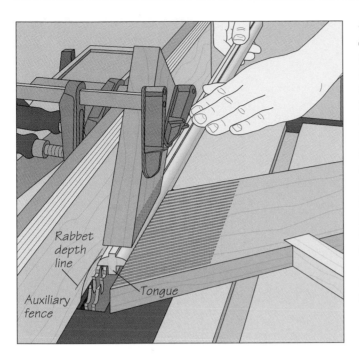

Rabbet depth line

Auxiliary fence

Tongue

2 Cutting rabbets for the glass panes

Install a dado head on your table saw slightly wider than the desired rabbets. The tongue remaining after the rabbets are cut should measure ⅜ inch wide. Install a wooden auxiliary fence and mark the rabbet depth on it—the combined thickness of the glass and the molding strip. Position the auxiliary fence over the dado head and raise the blades to notch the fence to the height of the marked line. Turn off the saw and mark the width of the rabbets on the leading end of the glazing bar. Butt one of the marks against the outer blade of the dado head, then position the fence flush against the bar. Use three featherboards to support the piece as in step 1, adding a support board to provide extra pressure to the featherboard clamped to the table. (Again in this illustration, the featherboard on the outfeed side of the table has been removed for clarity.) Feed the bars by hand *(left)* until your fingers approach the featherboards, then use the next workpiece to finish the pass. Complete the cut on the final workpiece by pulling it from the outfeed side of the table.

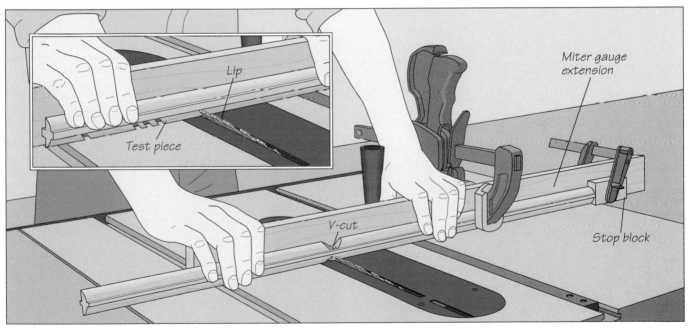

Lip

Test piece

Miter gauge extension

V-cut

Stop block

3 Making the miter cuts

Remove the dado head and install a crosscut blade. Adjust the blade angle to 45° and attach a miter gauge extension. To set the blade height, hold the extra glazing bar on the saw table so the tongue you cut in step 2 is flush against the extension. The top of the blade should be level with the lower side of the lip *(inset)*. Then mark the miter cuts on both sides of the bars; at their widest points, the Vs should be the same width as the stock. To make the cut, hold the tongue of the bar flat against the miter extension and align one of the marks with the blade. Butt a stop block against the end of the stock and clamp it to the extension for subsequent cuts. Clamp the workpiece to the extension and feed the glazing bar into the blade while holding it firmly in place. Rotate the piece and make the same cut on the other side of the V. Repeat the process to cut the V on the opposite side of the bar *(above)*.

4 Cleaning the V-cuts

Once all the miter cuts have been made, use a narrow chisel to pare away the waste. The width of the channel at the bottom of the V should equal the width of the lip. Holding the chisel bevel-side up, pare away the waste *(right)* until the bottom of the V is smooth and flat. Work carefully to avoid tearout.

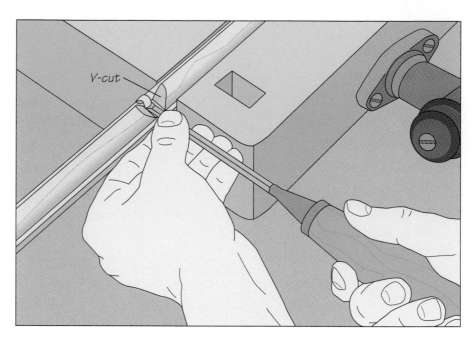

V-cut

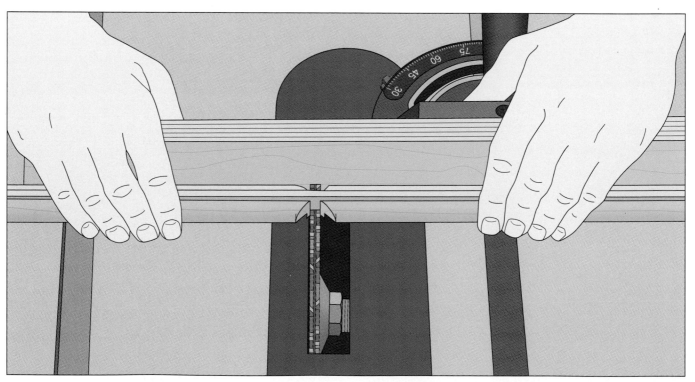

5 Cutting the half-laps

Reinstall the dado head in your table saw and adjust it to the width of the bar's lip. Set the cutting depth to one-half the stock thickness. You will need to saw a half-lap in the bottom of one glazing bar, then make an identical cut in the top of the mating piece. Set up the cut by aligning the middle of the V-cut with the dado head, while holding the bar flush against the miter gauge extension. Keep the work-piece flat on the saw table and flush against the extension as you cut the half-laps *(above)*. Use dowels or coping cuts *(page 66)* to secure the glazing bars to a frame-and-panel door, then install glass panes as you would for a glass-panel door *(page 69)*.

MOUNTING DOORS

Choosing the appropriate hinges for your kitchen cabinet doors depends primarily upon the style of cabinets you are building. Surface-mounted hinges, though limited in terms of weight capacity and ease of adjustment, are ideal for antique or rustic cabinets. Butt hinges *(page 76)*, available in iron or brass, are commonly used on flush-mounted doors and sit in shallow mortises cut into the door and case. Long, narrow cabinets often require piano hinges for strength and proper weight distribution. Tilt-out hinges *(page 77)* are practical for turning false drawer fronts into small, handy storage units.

When style is not an issue, and ease of installation and adjustability are more important, European-type cup hinges, or 32-millimeter hinges, *(page 74)* are an ideal choice. Fully concealed, strong, and simple to adjust once in place, cup hinges have become widespread in the homebuilding industry. Available for both European-style and face frame cabinets, cup hinges come with a variety of mounting plates that allow the installer to control the amount of overlay.

Before installing any hinge, read the manufacturer's instructions regarding placement. If you are working with fine, delicate woods, tap the stock for machine screws after drilling pilot holes to reduce the chance of splitting. A spot of glue in the hole will improve the holding ability of the fastener.

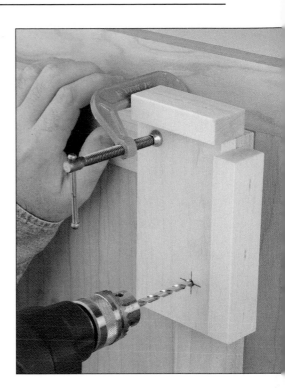

Locating doorknobs need not involve tedious measurement from door to door. The simple jig shown in the photo at right, made from a piece of plywood and two lips cut from solid stock, locates knobs in exactly the same spot on each door.

A SELECTION OF DOOR HINGES

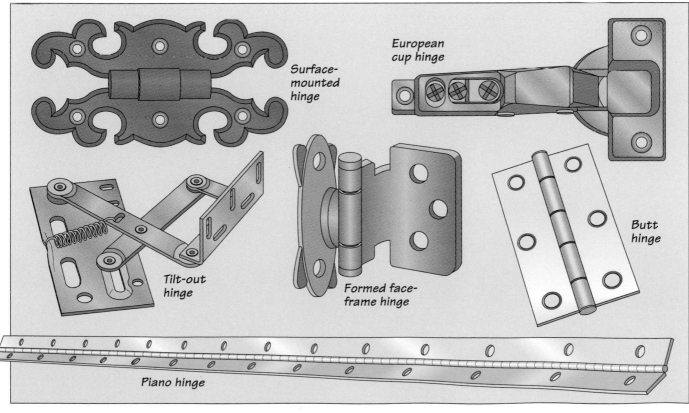

Surface-mounted hinge

European cup hinge

Tilt-out hinge

Formed face-frame hinge

Butt hinge

Piano hinge

MOUNTING AN OVERLAY DOOR

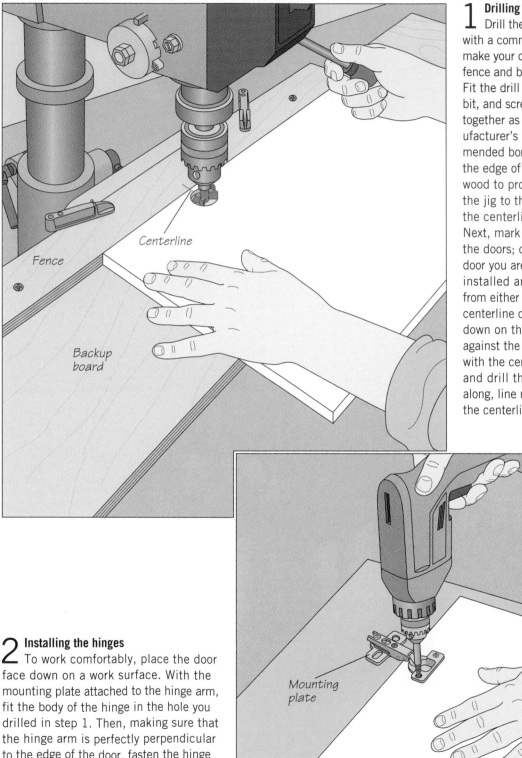

Fence

Centerline

Backup
board

1 Drilling holes for hinges

Drill the holes for European cup hinges with a commercial drilling jig and guide, or make your own jig by installing a plywood fence and backup board on your drill press. Fit the drill with a 35-millimeter Forstner bit, and screw the fence and backup board together as shown. Follow the hinge manufacturer's instructions regarding recommended boring depth and distance from the edge of the door; use a piece of scrap wood to properly position the jig. Clamp the jig to the drill press table, and mark the centerline of the hole on the fence. Next, mark the location of the hinges on the doors; depending on the size of the door you are working with, hinges can be installed anywhere from 3 to 6 inches from either end of the door; mark a similar centerline on the fence. Lay the door face down on the drill press table and butt it against the fence, aligning a hinge mark with the centerline. Hold the door steady and drill the hole *(left)*. Slide the door along, line up the second hinge mark with the centerline, and drill the second hole.

2 Installing the hinges

To work comfortably, place the door face down on a work surface. With the mounting plate attached to the hinge arm, fit the body of the hinge in the hole you drilled in step 1. Then, making sure that the hinge arm is perfectly perpendicular to the edge of the door, fasten the hinge in place with the screws provided by the manufacturer *(right)*.

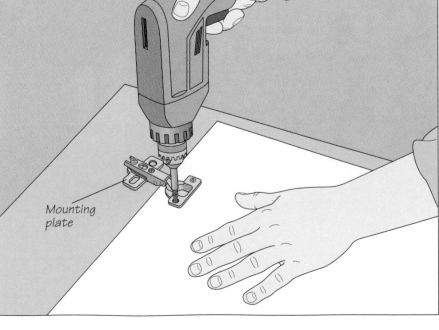

Mounting
plate

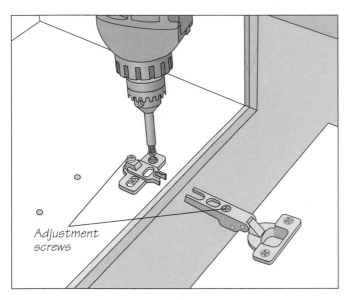

Adjustment screws

3 Installing the mounting plate

With the mounting plate still attached to the hinge, align the door with the cabinet as shown, and extend the hinge arms to butt the mounting plate against the panel. Making sure that the adjustment screws on the mounting plate are in mid-position, mark a reference line, unscrew the mounting plate from the hinge arms, and fasten it to the cabinet side (above). This need not be overly precise; the hinge can easily be adjusted after installation (step 4).

4 Hanging the door

Slide the hinge arms onto the mounting plate until they click into position (above), then screw them together. Close the door and check its position. Adjust the height, depth, or lateral position of the door by loosening or tightening the appropriate adjustment screws on the hinge arms and mounting plate.

INSTALLING EUROPEAN-STYLE FACE FRAME HINGES

Installing the hinge

European-style hinges are also available for face frame cabinets, the predominant cabinet style in North American kitchens. Install the hinges to the doors in the same manner you would an overlay door, but fasten the mounting plate to the inside edge of the face frame (left).

INSTALLING A FLUSH-MOUNTED DOOR

1 Routing hinge mortises

To rout the mortises for butt hinges on a flush-mounted door, first make a hinge mortising jig *(inset)*. Draw a centerline across the width of a piece of ¾-inch plywood and center a hinge leaf on the board's edge. Trace the profile of the hardware on the template. Next, install a straight-cutting bit in a router and rest the bit on the left edge of the hinge outline. Make a mark at the left side of the router base plate. Repeat the procedure at the right and inside edges of the outline. Use a square to complete the template profile and cut it out on a band saw. Now position the hinge on the cabinet side and measure the distance from the bottom of the cabinet to the midpoint of the hinge. Measure the same distance from the centerline of the template to either end of the jig and trim it to length. Finally, cut two small blocks for lips and nail them to the front of your template. To use the jig, place the cabinet on its side on a work surface, then set the router's depth of cut to the thickness of the hinge leaf. Butt the template against the bottom of the cabinet and clamp both in place. Using the template as a guide, rout the mortise *(above, right)*. Butt the template against the top of the cabinet and repeat the cut. Use a chisel to square the corners.

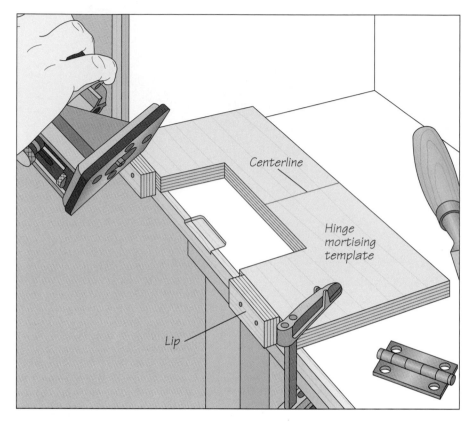

Centerline

Hinge mortising template

Lip

2 Hanging the door

To cut mating mortises in the edge of the door, secure the workpiece edge-up in a vise. Mark the hinge outlines on the edge of the door transferring their location from the cabinet side; make sure the hinge pin projects over the edge. Clamp an edge guide to the face of the door to provide a wider bearing surface for the router, then rout the mortises. Next, shim the door with a piece of wood so the door is level with the cabinet. Set the hinge leaves in the mortises cut in the cabinet sides, and screw the hardware in place *(right)*.

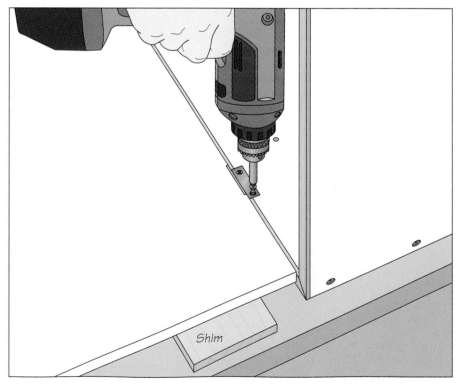

Shim

INSTALLING A TILT-OUT SINK TRAY

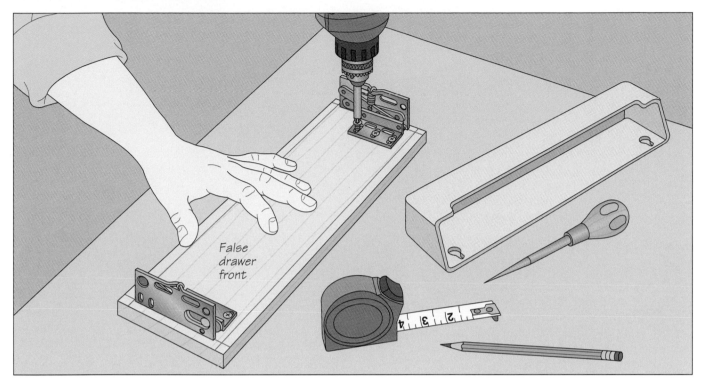

False drawer front

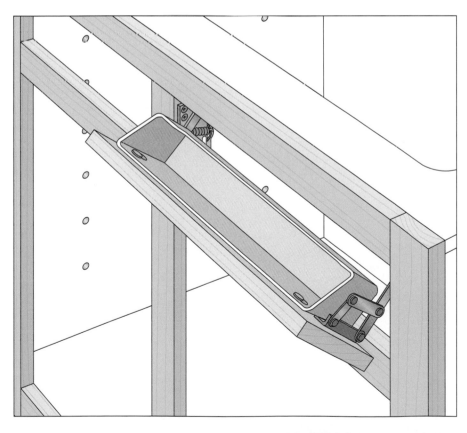

1 Attaching the hinges
A tilt-out sink tray is a handy space-saving fixture for storing soap, scouring pads, and sponges out of sight yet close at hand. To install the tray, first remove the false drawer front from the cabinet and place it on a work surface. Follow the manufacturer's instructions to trace the opening of the tray on the inside of the drawer front. Next, line up a hinge with the edge of the outline and center it on the drawer front. (When the hinge is closed, it will be in the middle of the drawer face.) Hold the hinge to the outline and screw it to the drawer front. Repeat the process for the other hinge.

2 Re-attaching the drawer front
Attach the two screws that hold the tray in place before installation. Then, making sure to spring the mechanism of the hinge first, line up the hinge in the middle of the drawer frame and screw the entire unit in place. Attach the other hinge, and hang the tray from the two screws.

DRAWERS

Properly proportioned and well-built drawers are an indispensable part of any kitchen. Like cabinet doors, well-styled drawer fronts can contribute handsomely to the overall look of a kitchen. Yet their appealing faces hide the kitchen's most abused elements: the drawers themselves. Their organization and construction are of paramount importance, for a visually striking kitchen can be a frustrating place to work if its drawers are haphazardly located or jam every time they are opened.

Kitchen drawers must be built to last. They are yanked open and slammed shut countless times a day. Worse, drawers in the kitchen are often weighed down with appliances and crammed full of cutlery and utensils, so any shortcut made in their construction will eventually compromise their strength and utility.

This chapter details the techniques involved in building strong, attractive, smoothly functioning drawers. The construction guides on pages 80 and 81 offer an overview of your options for drawer faces, joinery, mounting, and materials. Your eventual choice will depend on your experience, shop setup, and timetable. When it comes to joinery, there is little question that the strongest joint is the through dovetail *(page*

Drawers can influence look and feel of a kitchen. With their molded edges and round pulls, the bank of overlay drawers in the kitchen shown above speaks of a very traditional, almost Victorian, style.

83). Other options, like the lock miter *(page 37)*, dado *(page 35)*, and the double dado are suitable alternatives.

Kitchen drawers place tough demands on the mounting method used to secure them to the casework. Side-mounted full extension slides *(page 89)* are designed to withstand very rigorous use, and are the best choice if your budget permits. Bottom-mounted slides *(page 87)* are not quite as strong, but are less expensive and easier to install.

When it comes to the appearance of a kitchen, the front is the most important part of a drawer. The design of your drawer fronts will help set the tone for the kitchen's style. How well the drawers are installed will also prove to be a lasting testimonial to your craftsmanship. It can be a time-consuming task to hang a drawer so it rests perfectly straight and level, let alone several banks of drawers in a cabinet run. Applying a false front to the drawer *(page 93)* can reduce the time spent fussing with levels and drawer slides. With minimal experience, you can quickly and accurately install false fronts on both inset and overlay drawers. Even if the mounted drawers themselves are slightly uneven, they will appear to be hung with the precise eye of a master cabinetmaker.

A bank of inset drawers in a frameless cabinet like the one shown at left allows little room for error. By installing false fronts, the drawers need not be hung perfectly; the false fronts can then be positioned straight and level to the case.

DRAWER CONSTRUCTION

INSET DRAWER

Also known as a flush-front drawer, an inset drawer fits entirely within its cabinet. To hide the end grain of the drawer sides, a rabbet can be cut into the back face of the drawer front as shown above, or a false front can be added.

OVERLAY DRAWER

An overlay drawer features a separate false front screwed to the drawer front. A false front is typically larger than its drawer counterpart so that it overlays the face frame of the cabinet.

DRAWER JOINTS

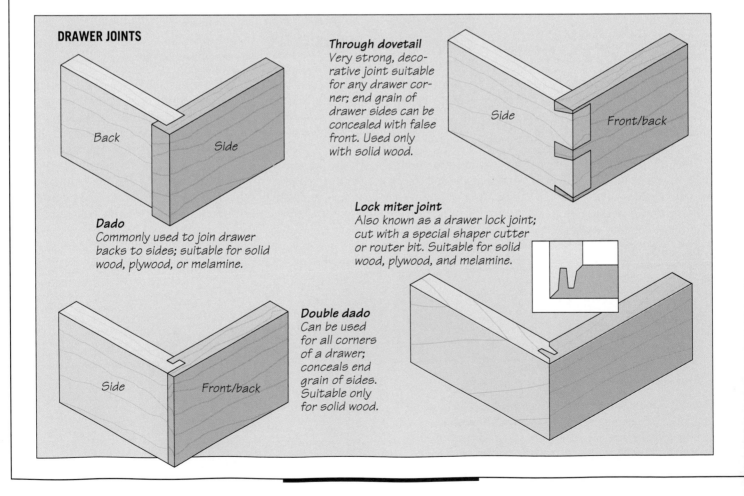

Through dovetail
Very strong, decorative joint suitable for any drawer corner; end grain of drawer sides can be concealed with false front. Used only with solid wood.

Dado
Commonly used to join drawer backs to sides; suitable for solid wood, plywood, or melamine.

Lock miter joint
Also known as a drawer lock joint; cut with a special shaper cutter or router bit. Suitable for solid wood, plywood, and melamine.

Double dado
Can be used for all corners of a drawer; conceals end grain of sides. Suitable only for solid wood.

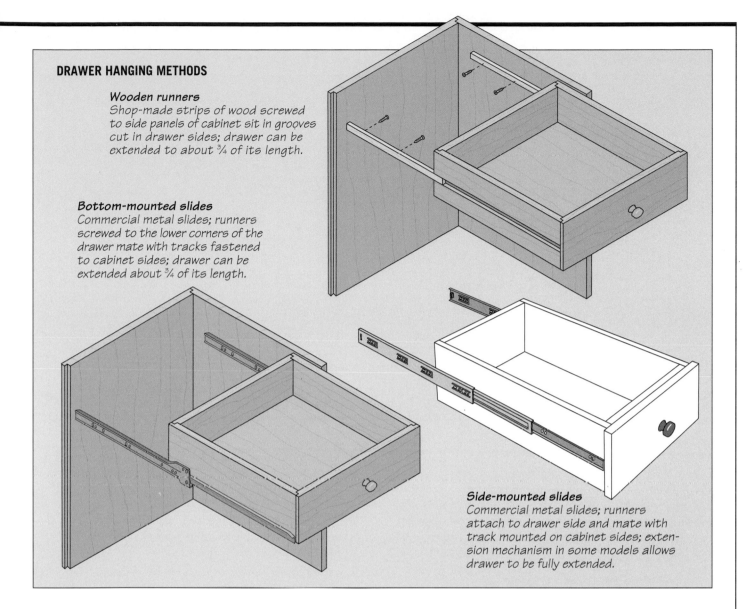

DRAWER HANGING METHODS

Wooden runners
Shop-made strips of wood screwed to side panels of cabinet sit in grooves cut in drawer sides; drawer can be extended to about ¾ of its length.

Bottom-mounted slides
Commercial metal slides; runners screwed to the lower corners of the drawer mate with tracks fastened to cabinet sides; drawer can be extended about ¾ of its length.

Side-mounted slides
Commercial metal slides; runners attach to drawer side and mate with track mounted on cabinet sides; extension mechanism in some models allows drawer to be fully extended.

MATERIALS FOR DRAWERS

MATERIAL	USES	COMMENTS
Solid wood	Sides, backs, fronts, false fronts	Use pine or other inexpensive wood for drawer carcase; save more attractive species for false fronts
Cabinet-grade plywood	Sides, backs, fronts, false fronts, drawer bottoms	Use plainsawn veneer for false fronts; trim edges of false fronts and top edges of drawer sides with solid wood banding *(page 48)*; use ¼" panels for drawer bottoms
Melamine	Sides, backs, fronts, false fronts, bottoms	Trim all edges with laminate edge banding *(page 49)*; use ¼" panels for drawer bottoms
Medium density fiberboard	Sides, backs, fronts, false fronts	Easy to work, yet fairly heavy for drawer construction; must be painted or veneered

PLANNING BANKS OF DRAWERS

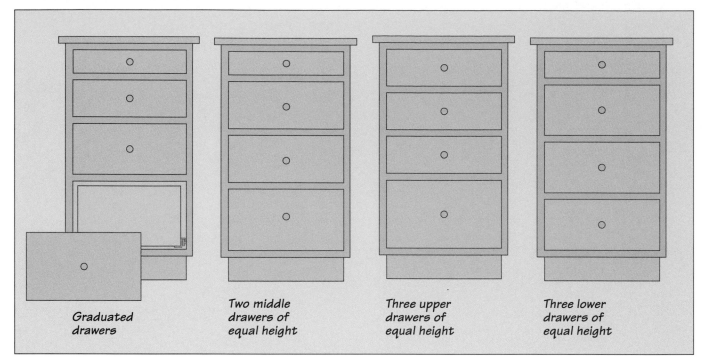

Graduated
drawers

Two middle
drawers of
equal height

Three upper
drawers of
equal height

Three lower
drawers of
equal height

Laying out a bank of drawers

There is only one generally accepted rule of thumb for planning drawer heights: a lower drawer should never be smaller than the one above. The human eye appreciates order in proportion; placing larger drawers atop smaller ones makes a cabinet look top-heavy. Otherwise, drawers are a matter of taste. Experiment with the designs shown above or take measurements from other kitchens you like. Once you have decided on a layout, mark the location of the drawers on the cabinet's story pole *(page 25)*. If your cabinets have face frames, use the chart below to calculate the size of the drawer pieces. For example, the width of a drawer side to be used with bottom-mounted runners should be ¾ inch less than the height of the drawer opening.

CALCULATING DRAWER DIMENSIONS

Subtract these amounts from the opening dimensions or cabinet depth.

PLANNING BANKS OF DRAWERS	HEIGHT	WIDTH	DEPTH
Side mounted runners			
With flush front	¼"	1"	¾" + thickness of false front
With overlapping front	¼"	1	
Bottom mounted runners			
With flush front	¾"	1	¾" + thickness of false front
With overlapping front	¾"	1	¾"
Wooden runners			
With flush front	¼"	⅛"	¾" + thickness of false front
With overlapping front	¼"	⅛"	¾"

BUILDING DRAWERS

Drawers tend to take a lot of abuse, so strength is of utmost importance when building them. A drawer that has been stapled together may look fine, and will even work well—for a while. But in a few years it will start to loosen, sag, and eventually fall apart.

When designing for strength, nothing tops the through dovetail joint. Many woodworkers remain intimidated by the degree of precision needed to execute this joint properly, yet commercial router jigs have placed this once-exacting task within reach of every cabinetmaker. If you do not have a router, the double-dado, a joint almost as strong as the through dovetail, can be cut on your table saw. Unfortunately, neither of these joints works well in plywood, one of the most common kitchen cabinet materials. For plywood, a lock miter (page 37) or dado joint can be used.

A lock miter joint is an easy way to turn out perfectly fitting drawer parts by the dozen. The joint features identical cuts in the end of one board and the face of the mating board. The steps for making a lock miter joint are shown on page 37.

CUTTING THROUGH DOVETAILS

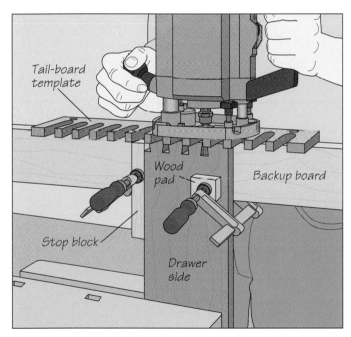
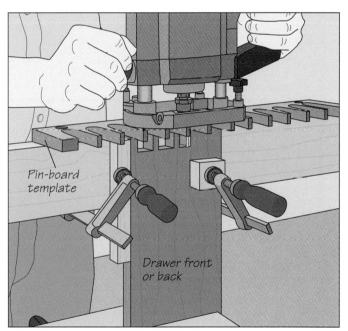

Routing through dovetail joints

When joining a drawer with dovetail joints, cut the pins in the front and back of the drawer, and the tails in the sides. To cut the dovetails with the commercial jig shown above, screw the pin- and tail-board templates to backup boards, then secure one of the drawer sides end up in a bench vise. Protecting the stock with a wood pad, clamp the tail template to the workpiece so the underside of the template is butted against the end of the board. Also clamp a stop block against one edge of the drawer side so the tails at the other end will match. Install a top-piloted dovetail bit in the router and set the depth to slightly more than the thickness of the drawer front. Cut the tails by feeding the tool along the top of the template and moving the bit in and out of the jig's slots *(above, left)*. Keep the bit pilot pressed against the sides of the slot. Repeat to rout the tails at the other end of the board and in the other drawer side. Then use the completed tails to outline the pins on the drawer front and back. Secure either one in the vise, clamp the pin-board template to the board with the slots aligned over the outline, and secure the stop block in place. Rout the pins with a top-piloted straight bit *(above, right)*.

DOUBLE DADO JOINTS

1 Cutting dadoes in the drawer front
Mark one end of the drawer front, dividing its thickness into thirds. Then, install a dado head on your table saw, adjusting its width to one-third the thickness of the drawer front. Set the cutting height equal to the thickness of the drawer sides. Next, install a tenoning jig; the model shown slides in the miter slot. Protecting the stock with a wood pad, clamp the drawer front to the jig; mark the outside face with an X. Move the jig sideways to align the blade with the middle third of the board. Turn on the saw and slide the jig along the miter slot to cut the dado. Turn the drawer front over and clamp it to the jig to cut the dado at the other end *(right)*.

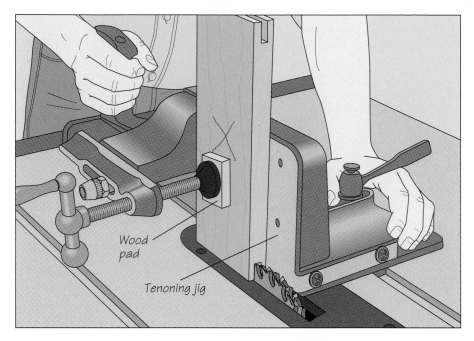

Wood pad

Tenoning jig

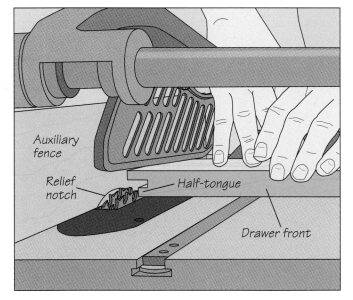

Auxiliary fence

Relief notch

Half-tongue

Drawer front

2 Trimming the tongues
Install a wood auxiliary fence on the rip fence. Mark a cutting line on the edge of the drawer front that divides the tongue on its inside face in half. With the stock flush against the miter gauge, inside-face down, align the mark with the blade. Butt the fence against the stock and raise the blades to cut a relief notch in the fence. Set the cutting height to trim the half-tongue. Holding the drawer front firmly against the gauge, feed it into the cutters *(above)*. Turn the board around and repeat the procedure at the other end.

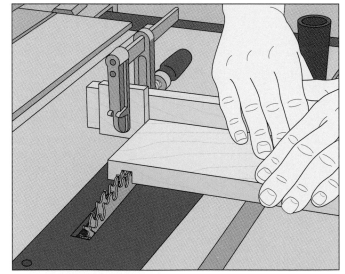

3 Cutting matching dadoes in the drawer sides
To join the drawer sides to the front, cut a dado near the front end of each side. The dado must mate with the half-tongue on the front. Set the cutting height to the length of the half-tongue and screw a wooden extension board to the miter gauge. To set the width of cut, butt the drawer side against the front and use a pencil to outline the half-tongue on the drawer side. Hold the side against the extension and align the marks with the dado head. Clamp a stop block flush against the end of the stock and feed the board to cut the dado *(above)*. Repeat the cut on the other side.

PREPARING THE DRAWER FOR A BOTTOM PANEL

Cutting the groove for the bottom panel
Dry-assemble the drawer and mark any spots where the joints bind; use a chisel to pare small amounts of wood to achieve a good fit. Next, use your table saw to cut a groove in the drawer front and sides to accommodate the bottom panel. Install a dado head, adjusting the width to the thickness of the bottom panel stock. Set the cutting height to half the stock thickness and adjust the rip fence to leave a ⅜-inch border between the bottom of the groove and the board edge. Feed the drawer front across the table using a push stick *(right)*. **(Caution: In this illustration the blade guard has been removed for clarity.)** Repeat the cut on the drawer sides. Finally, raise the blade height a bit higher than the stock thickness and rip the drawer back to width. This will allow the bottom panel to slide into position when the drawer is assembled.

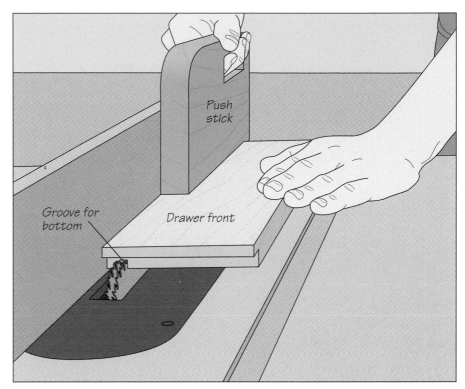

Push stick

Groove for bottom

Drawer front

ASSEMBLING THE DRAWER

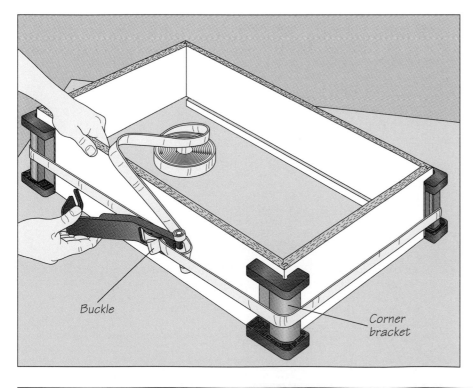

Buckle

Corner bracket

1 Clamping the drawer
A web clamp with corner brackets is ideal for gluing up drawers. The web distributes pressure evenly among all four corners, while the brackets help to spread the pressure along the length of each joint. To use the web clamps shown, apply glue to the contacting surfaces and assemble the drawer on a work surface. Next, fit the corner brackets in place. Wrap the straps around the drawer carcase and tighten them with the buckles before locking them in place *(left)*. When the adhesive has cured, remove the clamps and apply edge banding to the top edges of the drawer.

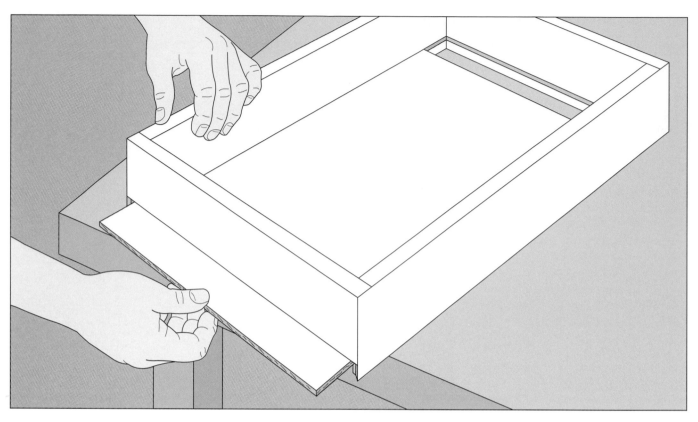

2 Installing the bottom

Trim the bottom panel $1/16$ inch narrower than the space between the two grooves. Slide the panel into place from the back *(above)*. Do not apply any glue. This will allow the drawer sides to expand or contract with changes in humidity; particularly if the sides are made from solid wood. Secure the bottom with a couple of finish nails in the drawer back.

SHOP TIP

Eliminating drawer rattle
Drawer bottoms always fit a tad loosely to allow for wood movement. Unfortunately, this can sometimes lead to an annoying rattle. An easy fix for this is to jam little wedges between the bottom panel and the drawer sides. Cut four to six wedges for each offending drawer. Be sure to cut them so the grain is oriented at a right angle to the taper. This will make it easy to break off. To install each wedge, tap it in place. Finally break off the excess by lifting the wedge.

Wedge

DRAWER SLIDES AND RUNNERS

Commercial slides have simplified the installation of drawers to the point where that they have virtually supplanted all other drawer-hanging hardware, and for good reason. The slides are simple to install and can be secured with only three or four screws. Some commercial slides even allow for fine tuning and can be adjusted vertically after the screws have been installed.

For the kitchen user, commercial drawer slides also offer unmatched durability. Good quality side-mounted slides *(page 89)* are rigorously tested; they must open and close flawlessly at least 100,000 times and support a load of 150 pounds when fully extended. Bottom-mounted slides *(below)* cannot bear nearly as much weight, but are considerably less expensive. Wooden slides *(page 91)* still have a placc. Inexpensive to make, they are perfectly suitable for light-duty situations.

Some bottom-mounted drawer slides can extend a drawer its full length to display the contents inside.

INSTALLING BOTTOM-MOUNTED SLIDES

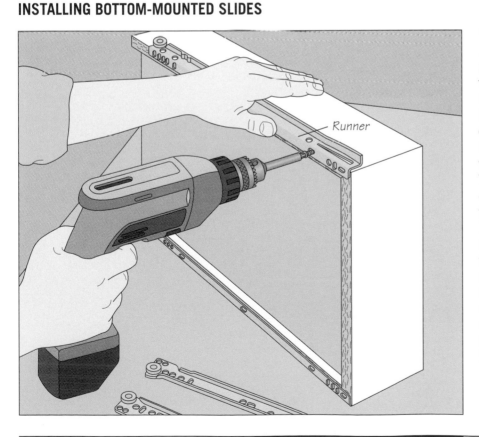

Runner

1 Attaching the runner to the drawer
Bottom-mounted slides consist of two parts: a runner that attaches to the bottom of the drawer slide and a track that is secured to the cabinet sides. Before installing the first drawer, place it in front of the case and lay out the slide parts beside it. Make sure you understand where each piece goes and its orientation. To position the runner, set the drawer on its side and butt the runner against the bottom of the drawer side as shown. Inset the hardware $\frac{1}{16}$ inch back from the drawer front so it will not interfere with the false front *(page 93)*. The runner can be secured from below or from the side. If you are using solid wood or plywood, attach it from the side. If you have chosen melamine, attach the runner from below *(left)*. In both cases, drill pilot holes first to avoid splitting the material.

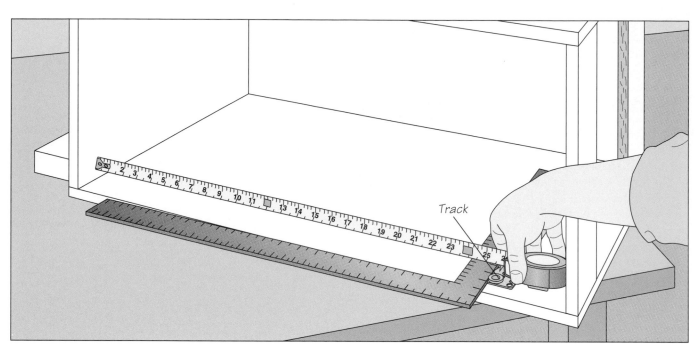

2 Positioning the tracks

Once you have determined the spacing of the drawers *(page 82)*, position the tracks for bottom-mounted slides on the sides of the cabinet. Place a track on the cabinet side, using a framing square to hold it at a right angle to the cabinet front. For face frame cabinets, place the track almost flush with the front edge of the cabinet; for frameless cabinets like the one shown above, inset the drawer by the thickness of the false front stock; typically about ¾ inch. Measure out the appropriate drawer height from the cabinet story pole *(page 25)* then move the square and track together to align the bottom of the track with this distance *(above)*. Given the combined thickness of the runner and track, this means the bottom of the drawer sides will be actually about ³⁄₃₂-inch higher than on the story pole. This bit of extra clearance over the drawer below will not be noticeable since the false fronts will cover the gap. Finally, mark the predrilled holes in the track onto the cabinet side.

3 Fastening the tracks

Drill a pilot hole at each of the marks you made in step 1, wrapping a piece of tape around the drill bit to ensure that the screws do not pass through the side of the cabinet. Then fasten the track in place with a screw in each hole *(right)*. If you have more than one drawer to install at a certain height, cut a plywood spacer to fit between the track and the cabinet bottom. You can use this to place all the tracks at exactly the same height without measuring. Repeat steps 1 and 2 for the other drawers in the cabinet.

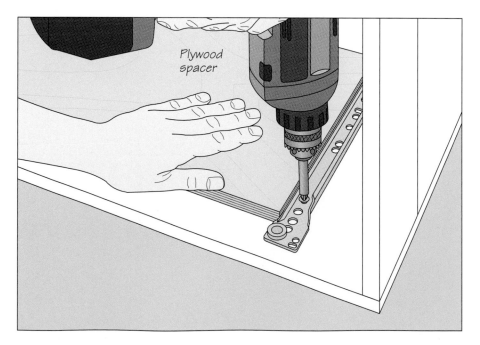

INSTALLING SIDE-MOUNTED SLIDES

1 Attaching the drawer runners
Unlike bottom-mounted slides, the runners of a side-mounted drawer slide can be attached to the side of a drawer at any height. To make installation easier, always offset the runner the same distance from the bottom edge of the drawer side. The runner in the illustration was placed 3⅛ inches from the edge, measuring to the center of the runner. Make a simple jig to position all the runners at exactly the same spot on each drawer. Fasten some one-inch-square stock as a lip to a 12-inch length of plywood, then trim the jig to width to hold the runner at the right position as shown. To attach each runner, first separate the runner from the track. Then clamp the jig to the drawer side and hold the runner against it, making sure it is flush with the drawer front. Secure the runner with screws *(right)*.

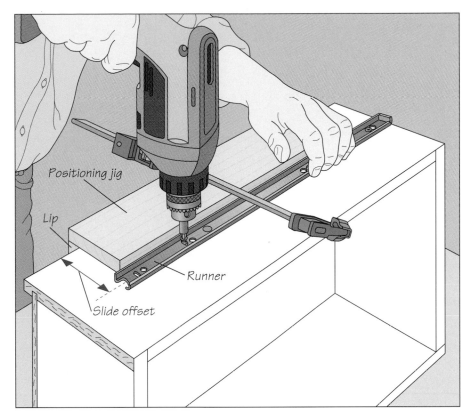

Positioning jig

Lip

Runner

Slide offset

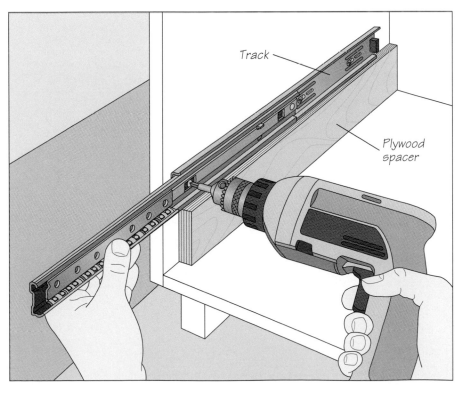

Track

Plywood spacer

2 Fastening the tracks
Position the tracks on the sides of the cabinet according to the desired spacing *(page 82)*. For the lowest track, simply measure the offset of the drawer runner *(above)* from the cabinet bottom, adding ¼ inch for clearance. Draw a line at this height. Hold the track against the cabinet side and center the predrilled screw holes over the line. For face frame cabinets, position the track so it is nearly flush with the front of the cabinet; for frameless cabinets, inset the track by the thickness of the false front stock. Fasten the track with screws *(left)*. The higher tracks can be positioned by adding the drawer height specified on the cabinet story pole *(page 25)* to the runner offset. Remember to measure to the center of the track. Repeat steps 1 and 2 for the other drawers.

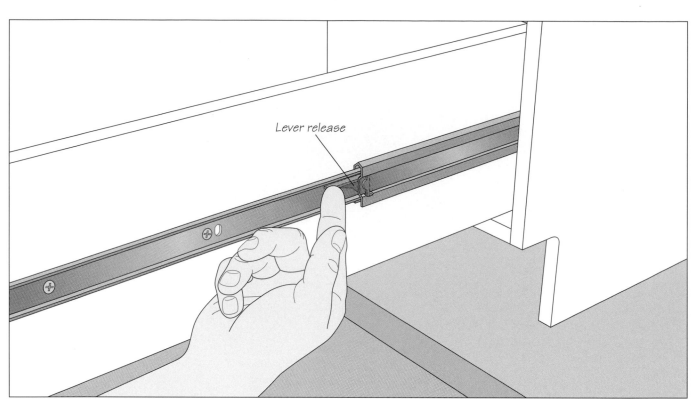

Lever release

3 Installing the drawer

If you have carefully positioned and installed the runners and tracks, the drawers can be hung by simply slipping their runners into the slides mounted on the cabinet sides. To remove the drawer, extend it fully then trip the lever releases on both slides *(above)*.

SHOP TIP

Building up face frame cabinets
Since most commercial drawer slides are designed to be screwed directly to the sides of a cabinet, they cannot be used on face frame cabinets without certain adjustments. Manufacturers make special brackets to bridge this gap but a much sturdier, shop-made alternative is to build up the cabinet sides. Rip some 1½-inch-thick solid stock equal in width to the distance between the edge of the face frame and the sides of the cabinet. You will need three upright pieces that stretch between the bottom and top of the cabinet. Drill pilot holes in the uprights every four to six inches. Locate each of the uprights so it is opposite a pre-drilled screw hole in the slide, then fasten the spacers to the cabinet side with wood screws. Now the slide can be securely installed in line with the inside edge of the face frame.

Long before the advent of commercial drawer slides, cabinetmakers were making simple yet efficient drawer runners from wood. The drawer in the face frame cabinet shown at right has dadoes cut into its sides that slide over wooden runners mounted to the inside of the cabinet. Four notched blocks screwed to the face frame and cabinet back support each runner. To install wooden runners in a frameless cabinet, see the steps below.

HANGING DRAWERS WITH SHOP-MADE RUNNERS

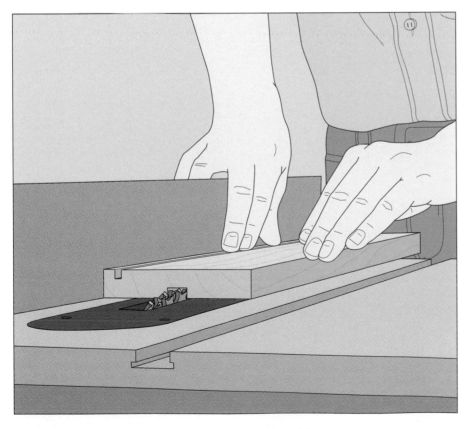

1 **Cutting grooves in the drawer sides**
Before assembling the drawer, cut a groove for the runner in the outside face of each drawer side. To make installation easier, offset each groove the same distance from the bottom edge of the drawer side. There are no rigid rules for the width of the groove, but it should accommodate slides that are thick enough to support the drawer. On your table saw install a dado head the same width as the groove. Draw cutting lines for the groove in the middle of the leading end of one drawer side. Also mark the depth of the groove; it should be no more than one-half the stock thickness. Butt the lines for the groove against the dado head, then crank the blades up to the depth line. Butt the rip fence flush against the stock and make the cut. Repeat for each drawer side.

2 Installing the slides

Mill the slide stock so its thickness and width are about ¹⁄₃₂ inch less than the dimensions of the groove in the drawer sides. Trim the slides a few inches shorter than the cabinet sides, then drill three counterbored clearance holes in each. Position the wooden slides as you would commercial side-mounted slides *(page 89)*. Hold a slide so it is inset from the front edge of the cabinet by the thickness of the false front stock, then screw it in place *(right)*. Test-fit the drawer. If it is too loose, add shims under the slides; if too tight, remove it and plane or sand it slightly thinner.

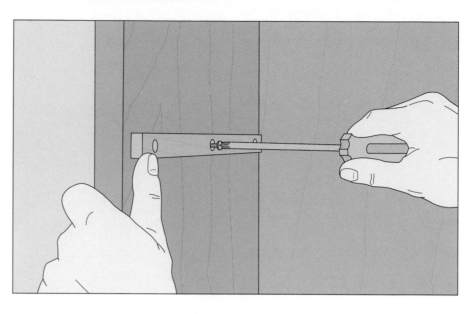

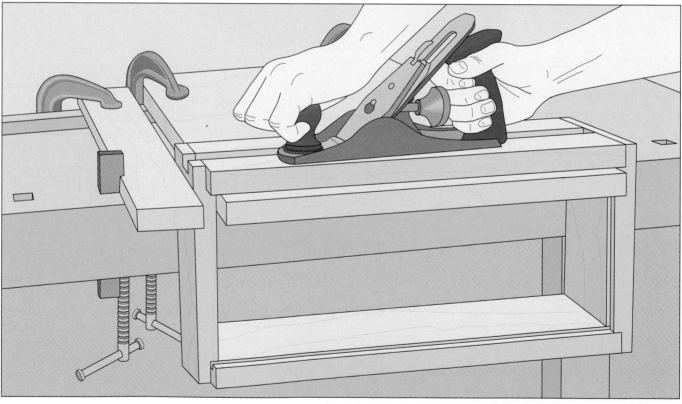

3 Fine-tuning drawer fit

Slide the drawer onto its runners. If the sides bind, remove the drawer and mark any shiny areas on the sides—high spots that can be shaved off with a hand plane. To secure the drawer for planing, clamp a wide board to a workbench with one edge extending over the side as shown. Remove the bottom of the drawer and hang the drawer on the board so the binding side is facing up. Then clamp another board to the workbench, butting it against the drawer; use a bench dog to keep the second board from moving. Gripping the plane with both hands, shave off the marked spots with smooth, even strokes *(above)*. Test-fit the drawer and repeat until it slides smoothly. Replace the bottom panel.

FALSE FRONTS AND HARDWARE

False fronts solve the problem of hanging drawers so they are perfectly straight and level. With the false front system, all the drawers in a cabinet are mounted as close to level as possible, then the fronts are positioned individually so they are plumb and level with the case or face frame. Shims are used to fine-tune the fit. The location of the false fronts are marked with nail tips set in the drawers, then the drawers are removed and the false fronts are fastened in place.

False fronts can be used with either frameless or face frame cabinets. The for-mer always uses inset drawers *(below)*, while the latter can have either inset or overlay drawers *(page 80)*.

Installing knobs or pulls is not tricky, but take the time to do it right. The key is to center the hardware on the drawer front. Techniques for installing the two different types of hardware are shown on page 97.

One of the final touches in making a drawer is adding the appropriate handle or knob. Here a drawer knob is attached to a frame-and-panel false front.

INSTALLING FALSE FRONTS ON INSET DRAWERS

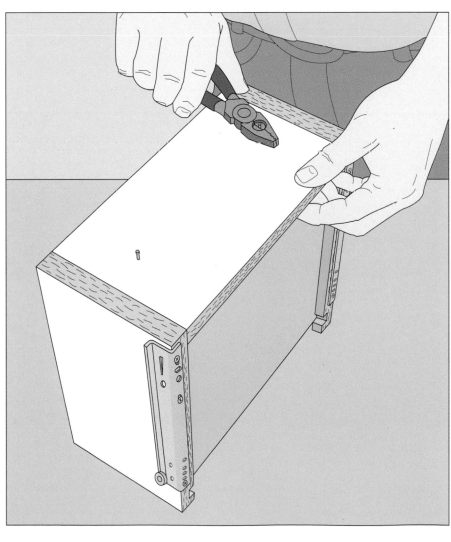

1 Preparing the drawer
Once the drawer slides have been properly mounted *(pages 87-92)*, set the drawer face-up on a work surface and drive two brads into the drawer front, leaving their head protruding. Make sure the brads are not located where the drawer pull will be installed. Then snip off the heads, leaving about ⅛ inch exposed.

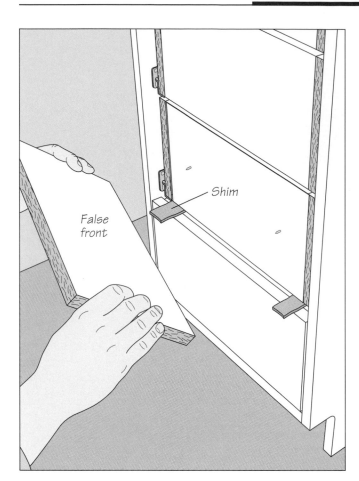

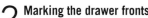

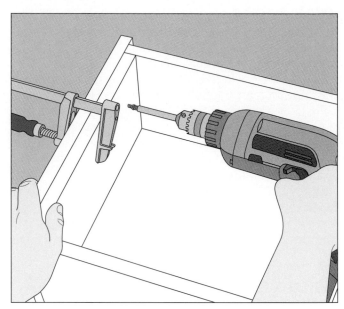

3 Attaching the false fronts

Apply a thin layer of glue to the front of the drawer. Position the false front in place, lining up the indentations you made in step 2 with the brad tips. Clamp the false front in place, then drill a pilot hole near each corner from the inside of the drawer; mark the proper depth on the bit with some masking tape to avoid drilling through the front. Finally fasten the false front with screws ¼ inch shorter than the total thickness of the drawer front (above).

2 Marking the drawer fronts

Install all the drawers on their slides. Starting with the bottom drawer, position its matching false front in place. Use paper or cardboard shims to level the false front and create an even gap of about ⅛ inch between it and the cabinet bottom. Pull out the drawer above to ensure that it clears the bottom false front; trim the front if necessary. When you are satisfied with the fit, push the false front into the drawer, driving the brad tips into the wood. Apply laminate edge banding (page 48) to the edges of the false front, then proceed to step 3 to install it. Mark the rest of the false fronts the same way, shimming each one against the finished drawer beneath it (above).

SHOP TIP

Sizing false fronts using two sticks
For cutting false fronts to size, two straight and square sticks can serve as accurate gauges for measuring the inside width of a kitchen cabinet. Place the sticks side by side in the cabinet, butting one stick against one side and the other against the opposite side. Mark a line across the sticks. Remove them and realign the marks. The combined length of the sticks will give you the correct measurement for the length of the false front.

INSTALLING FALSE FRONTS ON OVERLAY DRAWERS

1 Chamfering the false fronts
False fronts on overlay drawers typically have some sort of edge treatment, such as rounding over, chamfering *(shown here)*, or more involved shaping. First size the false fronts to match the drawer carcase front, plus the desired overlap. To chamfer the edges of the false front, install a piloted 45° chamfering bit in a router and mount the tool in a table. Align the fence with the bit's pilot bearing and adjust the height of the bit to cut all but ³⁄₁₆ inch of the front's edges and ends. Clamp two featherboards to the fence, one on either side of the bit, to hold the stock against the table. (In the illustration the front featherboard has been removed for clarity.) To reduce tearout, chamfer the ends before the sides. Feed the workpiece across the table with a push stick, using your left hand to press the stock against the fence *(right)*.

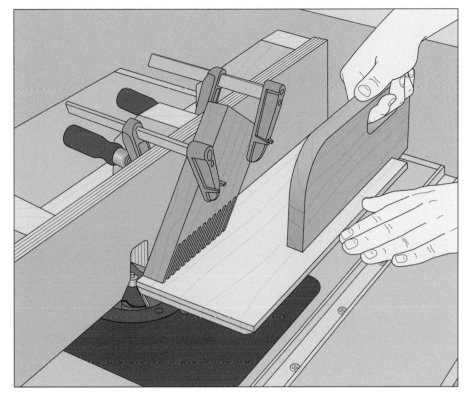

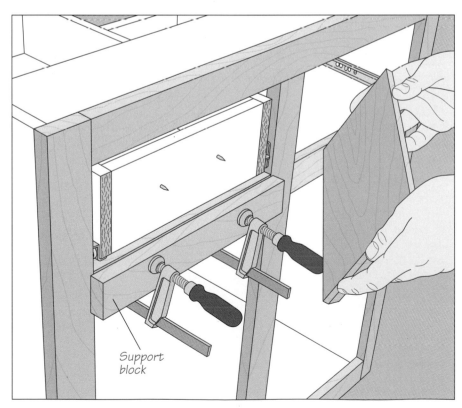

Support block

2 Marking the false front
Mark false fronts for an overlay drawer as you would for an inset drawer *(page 93)*. The example at left shows two side-by-side drawers over a pair of doors. A support block is clamped beneath the drawer to help position the false front in place. First prepare the front of the drawers by inserting and cutting off a pair of brads *(page 93)*. To place the support block, draw a line on the drawer rail where the lowest part of the false front will be. Clamp the block in place, then set the false front on top of it. Fine-tune the block's position by tapping it lightly with a mallet until the false front sits level and at exactly the right height. Then move the front right or left to center it horizontally. Finally, hold the front in position and push the drawer into the front to mark it *(left)*. The front can be screwed to the drawer *(page 94)* or glued in place *(page 96)*.

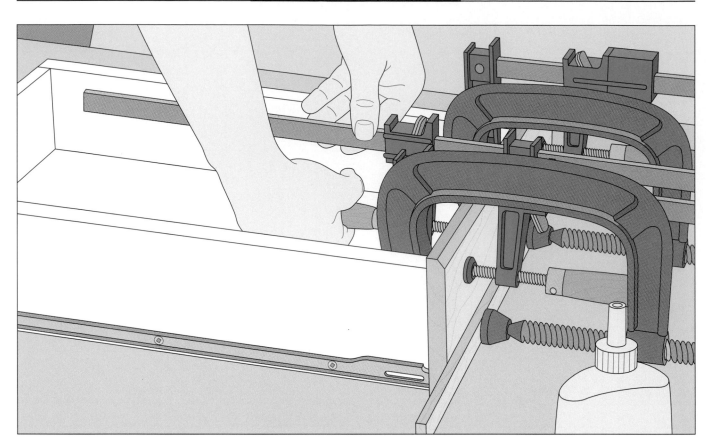

3 Gluing on false fronts

Remove the drawer and spread a thin layer of glue on the back of the false front. Place the front in position, with the two brads in their impressions. Hold the assembly together, using quick-action bar clamps along the edge of the front and deep-throated C clamps along the bottom edge; protect the stock with wood pads where necessary. Tighten the clamps evenly until there are no gaps between the false front and the drawer *(above)*.

SHOP TIP

Securing false fronts with double-faced tape
Double-faced tape is a quick and easy way to position and hold false fronts in place while installing them. Stick a strip of double-faced tape to the front of the drawer carcase. For face frame cabinets *(shown here)*, hold the false front in place with a support board. For frameless cabinets, shim the front with paper or cardboard shims. Then push the front against the drawer so it sticks to the tape. Finally, install the false front with screws.

HANDLES AND PULLS

1 Installing knobs
Drawers with single knobs should have the knob centered in the middle of the drawer front. To find the center, draw diagonals connecting opposite corners, marking just near the middle of the drawer *(right)*; do not make the lines too dark or they will be difficult to erase later. Drill a clearance hole for the knob; the hole should be just a shade larger than the bolt so the knob base will have something to bear against. Install the knob after applying a finish to the front.

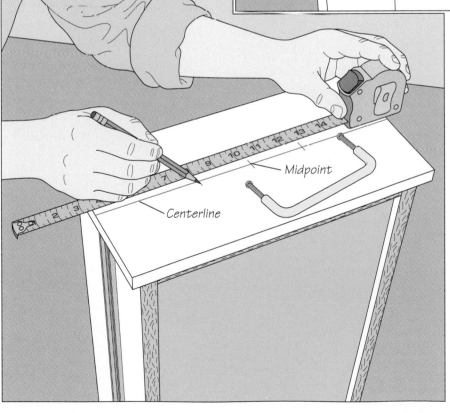

Midpoint

Centerline

2 Installing drawer pulls
The holes for drawer pulls are a little more time-consuming to mark. Most fronts are laid out so the pull is level and centered both horizontally and vertically; some taller drawers may have pulls placed a bit below the halfway mark. For a single centered pull, begin by drawing a line that divides the front in half lengthwise. Use a framing square to lay out the line, then double check with a ruler to make sure that it is even at both ends. Measure out the exact midpoint of this line and make a mark. Measure the distance from center to center of the two ends of the pull and divide this number in two. Mark out this distance on the centerline, measuring from both sides of the midpoint. Drill clearance holes through the front at these two points. Install the pull after applying a finish to the front.

INSTALLING CABINETS

A transfer scribe accurately follows the contours of a wall and draws a matching line onto a scribe rail. Once the rail is planed or sanded to this line, the cabinet will fit seamlessly when it is installed.

Installing kitchen cabinets can be the best of times, and the worst. Best, because it marks the completion of an arduous task; worst, because installation of perfect cabinets in an imperfect kitchen is sure to put your cabinetmaking skills to the test. Until now, you have worked on paper and in the relative calm of your workshop, carefully crafting your cabinets one by one. But a kitchen is not a workshop. When you bring your cabinets on site and start installing them, you may find yourself dealing with problems you had not anticipated, often working against the clock.

For example, no matter how painstakingly you have executed your story poles and built your cabinets to their specifications, there will undoubtedly be gaps between the carcases and the walls, floors, and ceilings. This is because the walls of a room, unlike your cabinets, are rarely straight. Fortunately, out-of-plumb walls can easily be straightened by adding additional rails to the end cabinets *(page 104)* and scribing them *(photo, above)*. The scribe rail can then be planed or sanded to conform to the wall.

The chapter that follows guides you through the steps and techniques necessary to install your kitchen cabinets and make sure they are plumb and level. A general review of installation techniques *(pages 100-101)* outlines several options for installing both lower and upper cabinet runs.

Pinpointing irregularities in kitchen surfaces is covered on page 102. Lower cabinet runs *(page 104)* are usually installed first, followed by the upper cabinets *(page 115)*. Some cabinetmakers, however, install the upper cabinets first, arguing that it is easier to do this task with the lower cabinets out of the way. While either option will work, stand-alone kitchen peninsulas and islands *(pages 112-114)* are best installed last, as they can create traffic jams during installation, no matter how well they are expected to work in the finished kitchen.

Placed on levelers, plinths, or their own integral bases, the lower cabinets *(page 104)* are shimmed from behind so their faces are plumb and aligned flush with each other, then the cases are fastened to the wall studs. Utility hookups such as hot and cold water supplies, drain pipes, and electrical outlets require special planning *(page 108)*. Before installing cabinets around such hookups, check with a professional plumber and electrician to ensure that the pipes are sound and the wiring is in good condition. Upper cabinets are mounted using nailer rails, European-style supports, or beveled wooden support rails *(page 115)*. As in the lower cabinets, variations in the length of a cabinet run may call for filler strips to bridge gaps between cabinets. The final touch is decorative crown molding *(page 118)*, which dresses the joint between the cabinets and the ceiling.

Positioning and installing the upper cabinets of a kitchen is more difficult than installing lower cabinets. Simple jigs such as shop-made cabinet jacks (left) *and temporary support rails* (page 115) *make the job much easier.*

When installing your kitchen cabinets, the technique you choose to keep them level will depend on your method of construction. If your lower cabinets feature an integral toe kick, you can use leveler legs *(page 44)* or shims *(page 106)* to position the cabinets level, plumb, and square with one another before nailing the cases to the studs. If your cabinets are simple carcases, leveler legs or a plinth base are both suitable.

While the plinth base *(page 112)* can be used with any lower cabinet, it is particularly well-suited to islands and peninsulas. This is because both of these cabinet types are difficult to secure to the floor while hiding the fasteners. The plinth is leveled first with shims or adjustable levelers, then fastened in place with a few L-brackets screwed to the floor and inside of the plinth. The island or peninsula is then screwed onto the plinth.

Upper cabinets can either be screwed to the wall studs through nailer rails *(page 116)*, specialized commercial hardware, or hung on beveled wooden support rails screwed to both the cabinet and the wall studs *(opposite)*. In both upper and lower cabinets, shims are used to level the cabinets and make them all appear to be a single unit seamlessly joined to the kitchen. Scribe rails and filler strips should take care of any gaps.

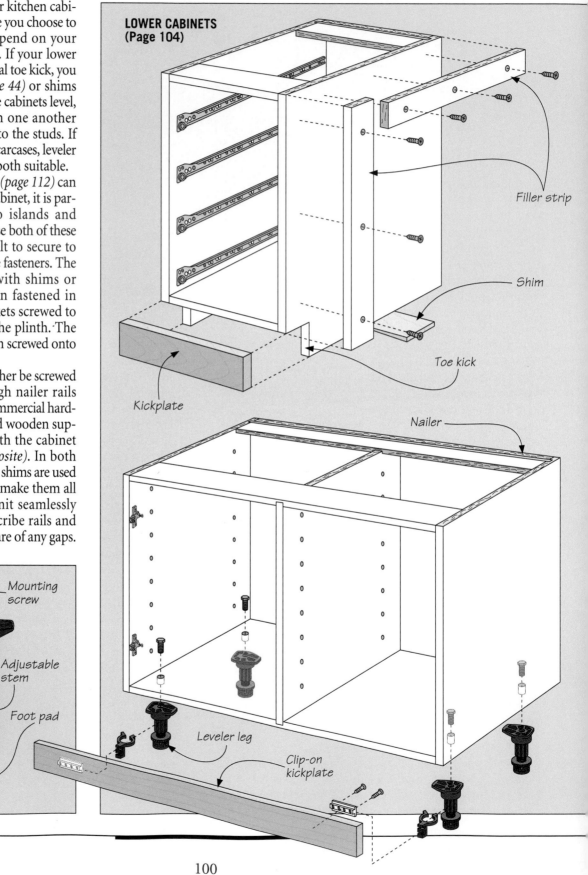

LOWER CABINETS
(Page 104)

Filler strip

Shim

Toe kick

Kickplate

Nailer

LEVELER LEG

Mounting screw

Cap

Toe kick clip

Adjustable stem

Foot pad

Mounting plate

Leveler leg

Clip-on kickplate

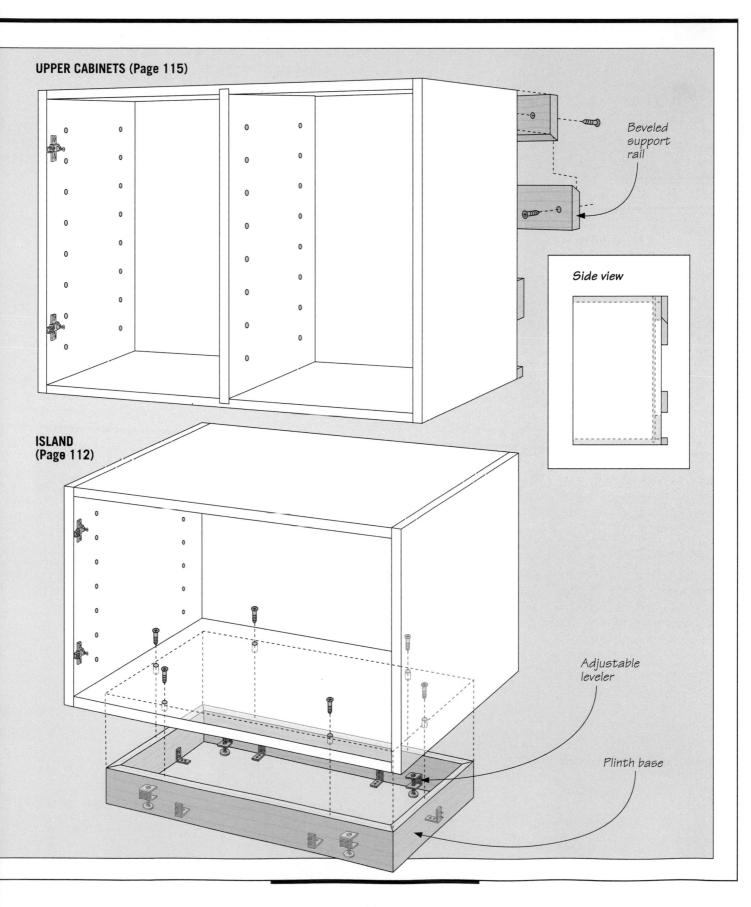

UPPER CABINETS (Page 115)

Beveled
support
rail

Side view

**ISLAND
(Page 112)**

Adjustable
leveler

Plinth base

The walls and floors of a kitchen are typically far from plumb, level, straight, and square. Common irregularities such as bows in the wall or a warped floor can create problems when it comes time to install cabinets that are perfectly square. In older homes, the studs in the walls may also be placed at intervals other than the standard 16-inch spacing used today. The best planned kitchen will pose installation challenges that cannot be tackled until the cabinets are ready for assembly on-site. However, you need to identify these irregularities

A chalk line simplifies marking out long level lines, such as indicating the top of a lower run of cabinets.

before you begin putting the cabinets in place.

Your first task is to draw level horizontal lines on the walls where the cabinets will go (below). If the kitchen floor is not level, you can adjust the height of the cabinets later with shims or various types of commercial levelers. Next, you need to locate the wall studs, which are crucial to securing the cabinets in place. This is easily done with an electronic device known as a stud finder, which detects differences in the thickness of a wall by means of a magnetic field.

Lastly, the squareness of corners will affect a close fit *(opposite)*. Scribe rails, used to cover gaps, must be wide enough to span any voids between cabinet sides and the adjoining wall.

PREPARING FOR INSTALLATION

1 Drawing layout lines
Use a long carpenter's level to draw a line on the wall at the height of the lower cabinets *(right)*. Measure this line from the highest point of the floor where it meets the wall *(page 24)*. If you have adjoining cabinet runs, start marking from the highest floor point of the respective walls. This ensures that you will only need to shim the cabinet bottoms to level the tops of the cabinets. (If you started from a lower point on the floor, cabinet bottoms would require scribing—a more laborious approach.) The lines can also be easily laid out with a chalk line *(photo, above)*. Repeat the procedure to mark the bottom of the upper cabinets.

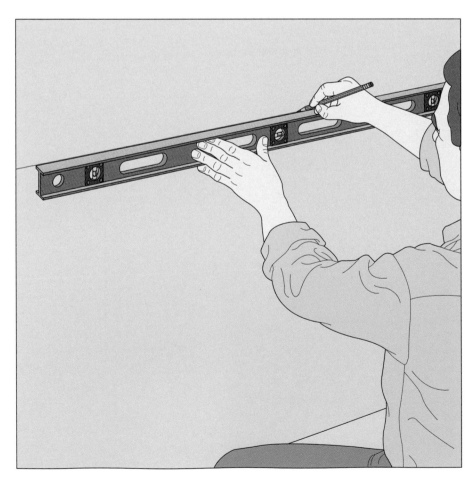

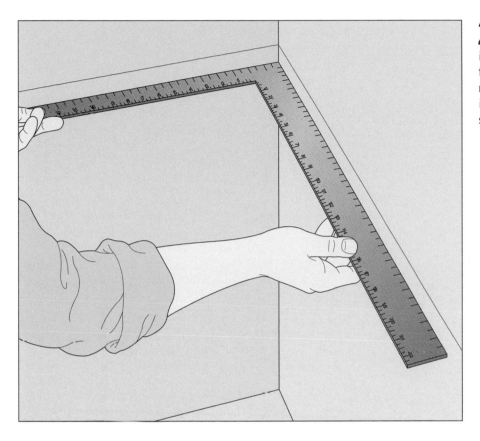

2 Checking the corners for square
Use a carpenter's square to determine if a corner is square *(left)*. If not, measure the gap, and use this figure to make scribe rails *(page 104)*. Use a plumb bob to see if the wall leans inward. If it does, measure the gap at its widest point.

3 Locating wall studs
Use an electronic stud finder to locate the centers of the studs in the walls. Following the manufacturer's instructions, calibrate the sensor and place the device against the wall. Press the operating button and slide the sensor sideways across the wall *(below)*; the red light will come on as the device passes over a stud. Determine the edges of each stud and mark its center. You can also snap a chalk line up the center of each stud to locate it for both upper and lower cabinets.

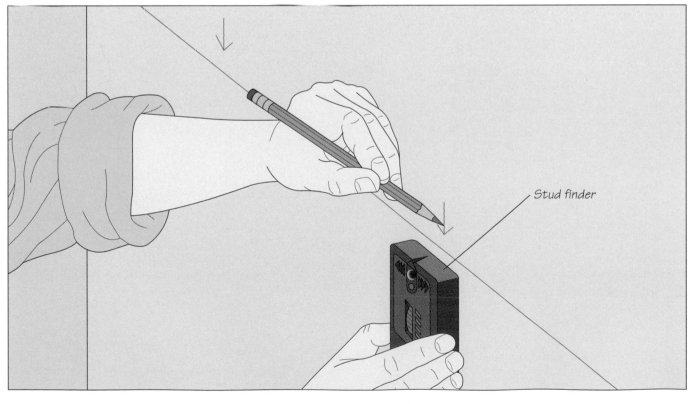

Stud finder

INSTALLING A LOWER CABINET RUN

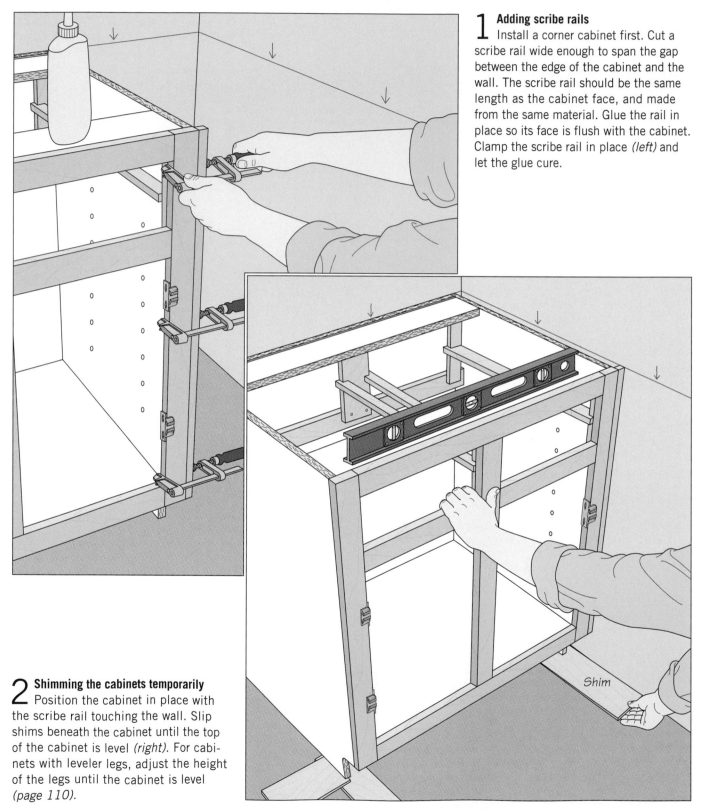

1 Adding scribe rails

Install a corner cabinet first. Cut a scribe rail wide enough to span the gap between the edge of the cabinet and the wall. The scribe rail should be the same length as the cabinet face, and made from the same material. Glue the rail in place so its face is flush with the cabinet. Clamp the scribe rail in place *(left)* and let the glue cure.

2 Shimming the cabinets temporarily

Position the cabinet in place with the scribe rail touching the wall. Slip shims beneath the cabinet until the top of the cabinet is level *(right)*. For cabinets with leveler legs, adjust the height of the legs until the cabinet is level *(page 110)*.

Shim

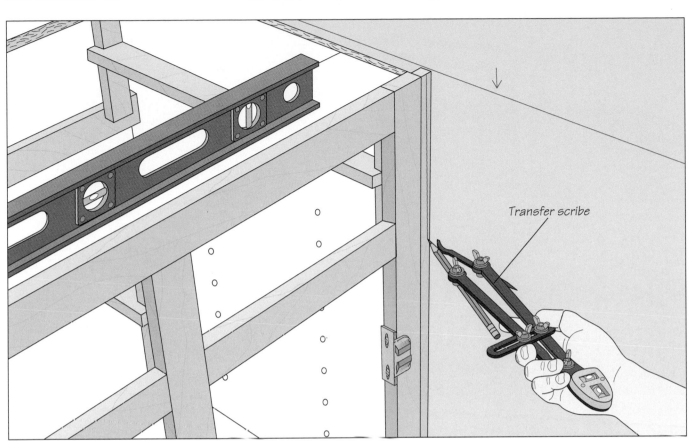

Transfer scribe

3 Scribing the rail
Set a transfer scribe slightly larger than the gap you determined for the scribe rail *(page 103)*. Place the steel point against the wall and lay the pencil point on the scribe rail. Keep the two points level as you slide the transfer scribe down the wall *(above)*, marking the contour of the wall on the rail.

4 Planing the scribe rails
Sand or plane the edge of the scribe rail down to the line you scribed in step 2. Tilt the tool a bit toward the rear of the cabinet as you plane the scribe rail, creating a slight bevel *(left)*. This bevel need not be very pronounced, but will ensure a snug fit when the cabinet is installed.

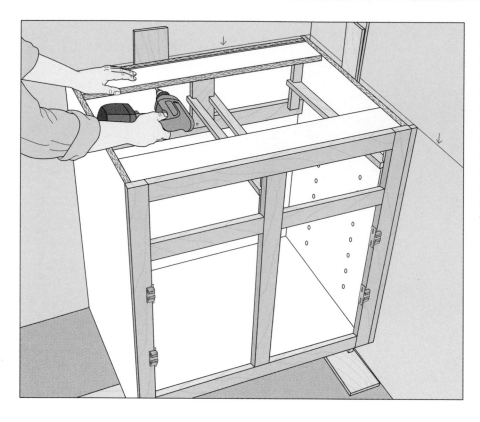

5 Installing the cabinet
Reposition the cabinet in place with the scribe rail touching the wall. Shim the bottom and sides of the cabinet so it is level and its top is aligned with the reference line on the wall. Fasten the cabinet in place by screwing through the shims and rear nailers into the wall studs *(left)*. Trim the excess from the shims with a sharp knife. Align the next cabinet in the run and screw it to the first cabinet *(below)*. Repeat to install the remainder of the run.

INSTALLING ADJACENT RUNS

1 Aligning adjacent cabinets
To install runs of cabinets on adjacent walls, start with the corner cabinet. Level and install the case as you did in step 5 *(above)*, then align the next cabinet. Place and adjust shims as needed so the cabinet faces are flush and level. Clamp the cabinets together in position *(right)*.

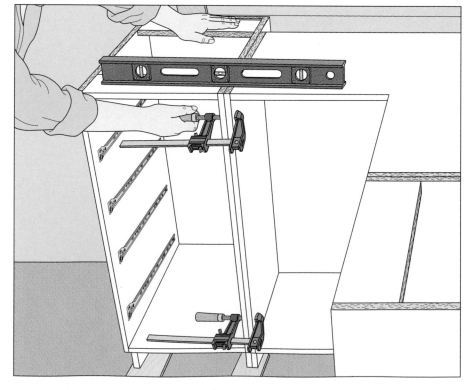

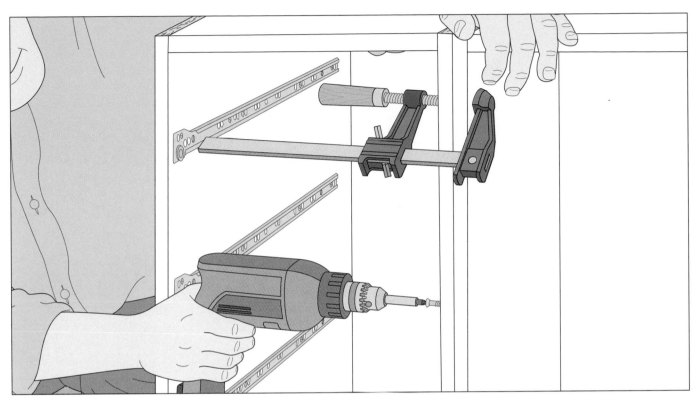

SHOP TIP

Making thick shims
If you must shim a wide gap, add a sufficiently thick piece of plywood to a standard cedar shim. This eliminates the need for several shims, which may shift and complicate the leveling process. Using a piece of plywood of uniform thickness also ensures that the shim will not introduce additional irregularities, as may happen when placing many shims next to each other. Join the shim to the plywood with a short screw; make sure the head of the fastener is sunk below the surface of the shim.

2 Fastening the cabinets
Once you have aligned the cabinets, fasten them together with screws. Drill three countersunk pilot holes at the front and the back of one cabinet side. If you are using ¾-inch-thick stock for your cabinets, make these holes 1¼ inches deep. Then drive the fasteners in place *(above)*.

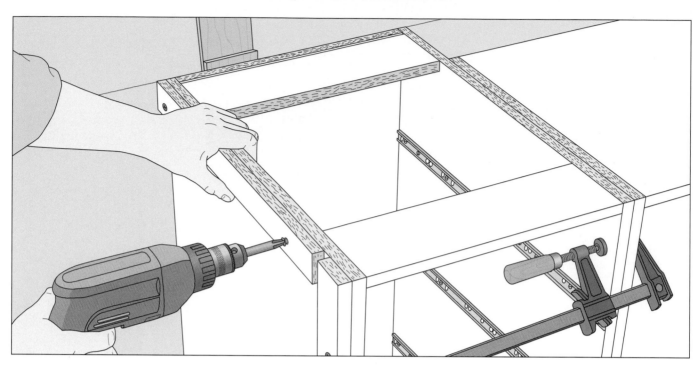

3 Installing filler strips

Minor aberrations in the measurement of the walls and cabinets can leave you with a gap between the last cabinets to be installed. If the space cannot be eliminated by adding scribe rails of equal width at either end of the run, cut a filler strip the length of the cabinet face and wide enough to bridge the gap between the two cabinets. Cut the piece from the same material as the cabinets, then screw it to the cabinet already installed. Screw an additional strip along the top edge of the cabinet *(above)*, as wide as the front filler strip and as long as the depth of the cabinets. Slide the next cabinet in place, and install it as in step 2.

FITTING CABINETS AROUND UTILITY HOOKUPS

1 Locating utility cutouts

Using the cabinet story poles for the appropriate cabinet *(page 24)*, transfer the measurements for plumbing and electrical outlets onto the back panel of the cabinet *(right)*. Indicate the position and size of each utility cutout.

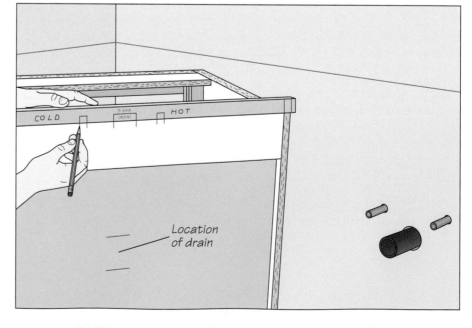

COLD   B-SINK DRAIN   HOT

Location of drain

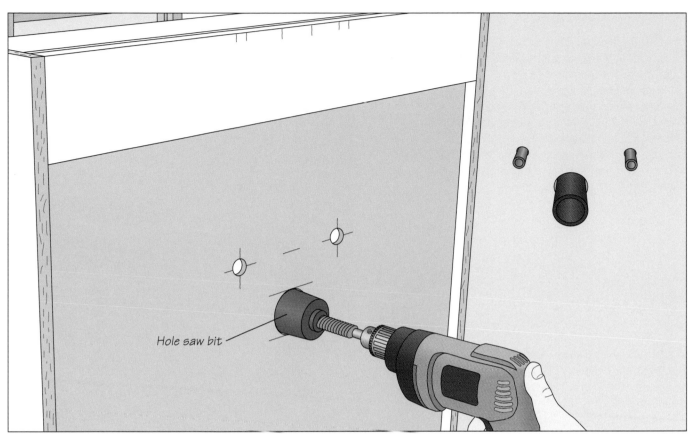

Hole saw bit

2 Cutting holes

Cut the holes using a drill fitted with a hole saw the same size as the cutout *(above)*. Make the holes slightly larger than the pipe. A keyhole saw can be used for larger holes.

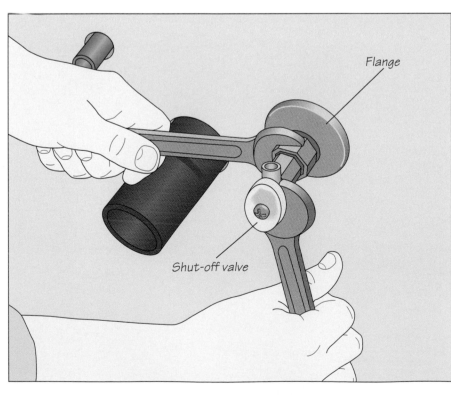

Flange

Shut-off valve

3 Attaching shut-off valves

Fit decorative flanges over the pipes, then fasten shut-off valves to the pipe ends. These taps usually require only wrenches *(left)* to fasten them in place. A flexible supply tube then feeds the water to the taps.

INSTALLING KICKPLATES

1 Leveling the cabinet
If your cabinets have integrated toe kicks *(page 100)*, proceed to step 2. For cabinets with leveler legs, use a level to guide you while you adjust the legs *(right)*. Shift the level from the front to the side and repeat as necessary until the cabinet is level on all sides. Secure the cabinet in place by driving fasteners through the nailers into the wall studs.

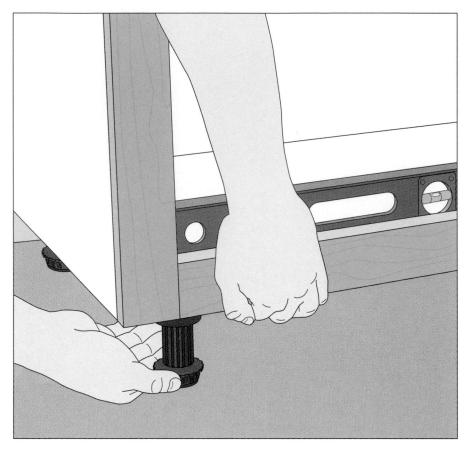

2 Scribing the kickplate
To fit the kickplate, place it on the floor in front of the cabinet *(below)*. Use a transfer scribe to scribe the kickplate as you did the scribe rail *(page 105)*. The top edge of the kickplate should be level; use shims if necessary. Plane the kickplate to the line.

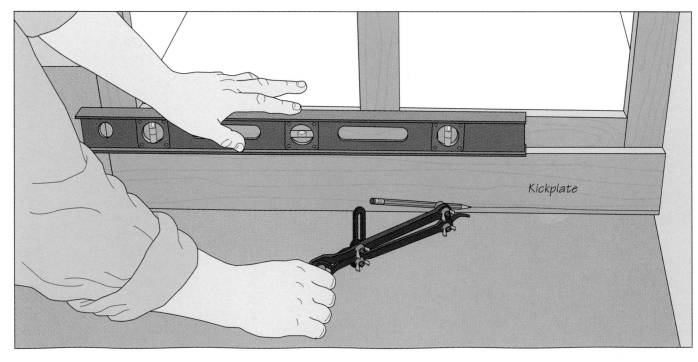

Kickplate

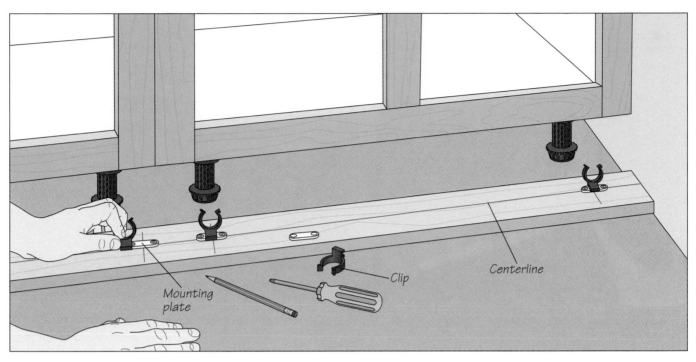

Mounting plate

Clip

Centerline

3 Fitting the retaining clips
Draw a centerline down the length of the kickplate's inside face. Indicate the location of each leveler leg on the kickplate. Screw the rectangular mounting plates at each of these points, then slide the clips onto the mounting plates *(above)*.

4 Attaching the kickplate
Line up the clips with the legs *(left)* then snap the kickplate in place. Slide the clips slightly along the mounting plates, if necessary, so they line up with their respective legs when the kickplate is properly positioned.

ISLANDS AND PENINSULAS

If your kitchen is large enough, the addition of a freestanding island can tighten work triangles, reduce kitchen traffic, and eliminate countertop clutter. Incorporating a sink or range and additional storage space into the island can improve the overall efficiency of your kitchen even more.

Installing a kitchen island requires a different approach than the one used for kitchen cabinets, as the island has no support from the walls. One solution is to set the island on a plinth. This is a wooden frame with a perimeter slightly smaller than the cabinet. The plinth is assembled with splined miter joints, leveled, and fastened to the floor; the island cabinet is then screwed to the plinth. The plinth can be made from plywood or solid wood. The former is recommended if the floor is uneven; separate kick-plates can be scribed and added later.

With its large tiled countertop, sink, and ample storage below, the kitchen island above does double duty as a dishwashing and food preparation area. Instead of resting on a plinth, the island is set on a molded base frame.

INSTALLING A KITCHEN ISLAND

1 Preparing the frame pieces

Assemble the plinth from veneered ¾-inch plywood or solid stock using splined miter joints at the corners. First, rip the four frame pieces to width—typically, 4 inches. To cut the frame pieces to length, tilt the table saw blade to 45° and miter the ends; when assembled, the plinth should be inset 3 inches from all sides of the island cabinet. Next, make some splines from ¼-inch plywood; they should be as long as the width of the frame pieces and ½ inch wide. To cut the grooves in the frame pieces for the splines, remove the saw blade and install a dado head set to the thickness of the splines. Adjust the height of the saw blade so it cuts a 45° dado into the mitered end of the frame pieces *(right)*; the depth of the dado should be half the width of the splines.

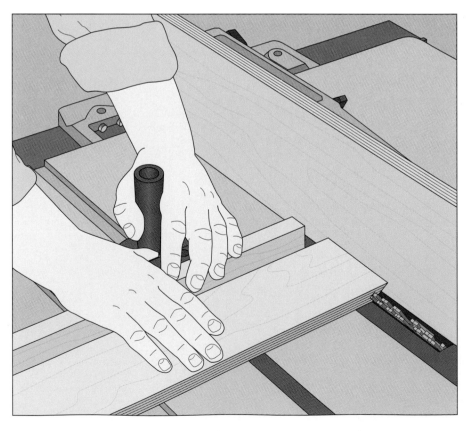

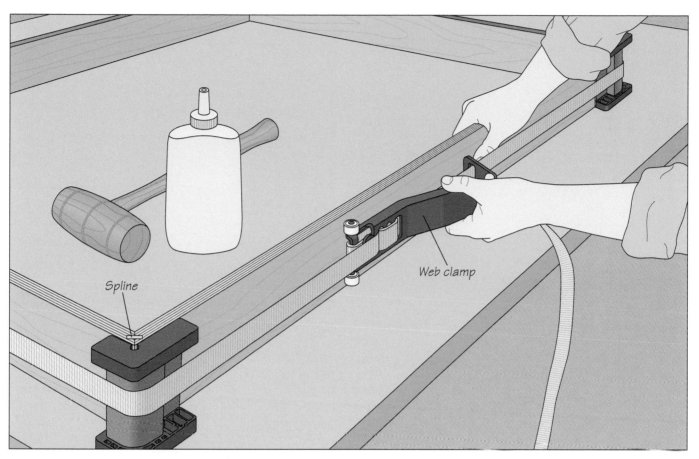

Spline

Web clamp

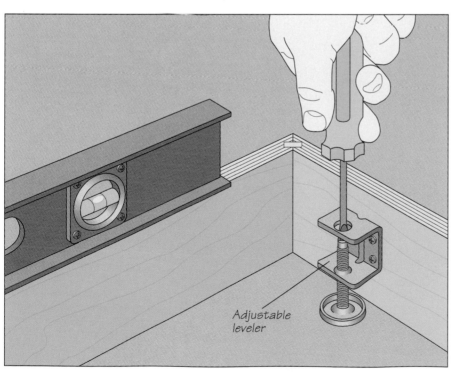

Adjustable leveler

2 Assembling the plinth

Apply glue to the ends of the frame pieces, spreading it in the dadoes you cut in step 1. Spread adhesive on the splines and tap them into the dadoes. Assemble and clamp the plinth using a large web clamp *(above)*; the model shown features special corners that distribute the clamping pressure evenly along the miter joints.

3 Leveling the plinth

Screw an adjustable leveler at each corner of the plinth, installing the first one at the highest floor elevation of the four corners. Set this leveler as low as possible, then raise or lower the others as needed until the top of plinth is level *(left)*.

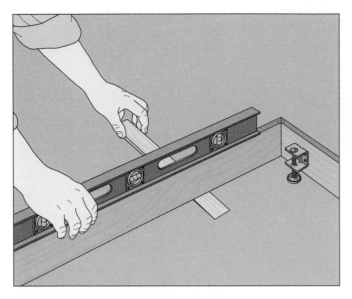

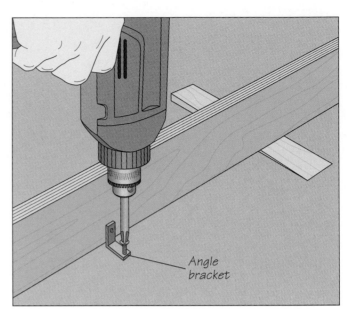

Angle
bracket

4 **Shimming the plinth**
If the floor is uneven, you will undoubtedly end up with gaps between the bottom of the plinth and the floor once the plinth has been leveled. Fill the gaps with shims, positioning each one so its wide end is outside the plinth area *(above)*. Add a drop of glue to each shim to hold it in place, and use a carpenter's level to ensure that you do not shift the plinth as you insert additional shims.

5 **Fastening the plinth to the floor**
Fasten the plinth to the floor using L-shaped angle brackets. Set the brackets in place and screw them to the inside face of the plinth; use two brackets per side. Then screw the hardware to the floor *(above)*. Once the plinth has been fastened in place, cut the shims flush with the outside face of the plinth.

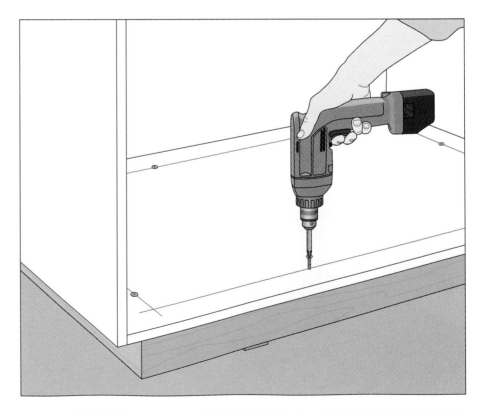

6 **Installing the island cabinet**
Center the island cabinet on the plinth, and mark out the position of the plinth on the cabinet bottom. Screw the cabinet in place *(right)*, driving the fasteners through the cabinet bottom into the plinth. After the cabinet is in place, scribe and install kickplates *(page 110)* on the outside faces of the plinth.

INSTALLING THE UPPER CABINETS

Upper cabinets can be fastened to the walls in one of three ways. The easiest method is simply to screw the cabinets to the wall studs through nailers *(below)*. If you want a less permanent solution, you can hang the cabinets from shop-made interlocking rails *(page 116)*. One rail is screwed to the back of the cabinet, the other to the wall. Cabinets can also be hung using commercially available adjustable rails and cabinet supports *(photo, right)*. Whatever method you choose, the cabinets need to be leveled before final installation.

The European-style cabinet support shown in the cutaway cabinet at right provides stronger support for mounting upper cabinets than screws driven into the wall. Screwed to the inside corner of a cabinet, the hardware features a metal hook that protrudes through the back and clips onto a rail fastened to the wall behind the cabinet. Adjustment screws allow the cabinet to be leveled and tightened against the rail.

INSTALLING UPPER CABINETS

1 Installing a temporary support rail
Attaching a temporary support rail will help you hold the upper cabinets in position as you install them. Screw a straight piece of 1-by-2 stock to the wall *(above)*, aligning its top with the layout line indicating the bottom of the upper cabinet run. Make sure to drive the fasteners into the wall studs.

2 Installing the first cabinet
Position the first cabinet in the upper run in its corner, setting it on the support rail. If necessary, add a scribe rail *(page 105)*, then reposition the cabinet and screw it to the wall studs with two screws driven through the back of the cabinet near the top. Do not drive the fasteners all the way; leave some slack so you can shim the cabinet. Clamp a level to the side of the cabinet and slip shims behind the case until it is plumb *(left)*, then tighten the screws. Drive a second pair of screws into the wall studs through the back of the cabinet at the bottom.

3 Installing additional cabinets
Position the second cabinet in the run next to the first and clamp them together so the faces are flush. Drive two screws in the second cabinet *(right)*, leaving them slack so you can shim the cabinet as in the previous step. Shim the second cabinet until it is level, then screw it to the first cabinet. Tighten the screws joining the second cabinet to the wall. Screw the cabinets together. Repeat to install the other cabinets in the run.

USING BEVELED NAILERS

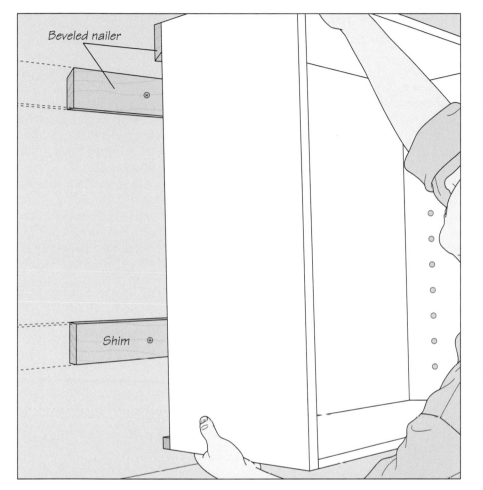

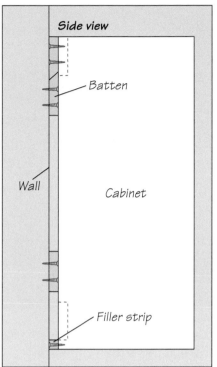

Side view

Batten

Wall

Cabinet

Filler strip

Hanging the cabinets

If you are using beveled nailers to install your cabinets, first screw a length of 1-by-6 to the back of an upper cabinet. Position the case on the wall so the bottom of the case is aligned with the line on the wall indicating the bottom of the upper cabinets, then mark the location of the 1-by-6 on the wall. Remove the strip of wood and cut a 45° bevel down its middle. Crosscut the pieces to the desired length. Screw one of the strips to the wall studs as a batten, its bevel pointing up and facing the wall. Screw the other piece to the back of the cabinet as shown. Attach a second rail an equal distance from the bottom of the cabinet to act as a shim. Screw a filler strip to the back of the cabinet flush with the bottom, then hang the case in place *(top, left)*.

SHOP TIP

Shop-made cabinet jacks

Cabinet jacks serve as an extra pair of hands, holding a case in place while you install it. You can easily make your own shop-built jacks. Simply screw three pieces of plywood or melamine together into the I-shape shown at right. Make the pieces as long as the distance between the upper cabinets and the countertop. The center piece should be wide enough to support a cabinet unit.

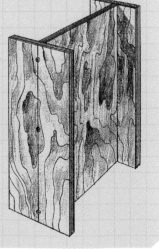

CROWN MOLDING

C rown molding adds a nice finishing touch to a set of kitchen cabinets. It can also hide uneven ceilings and visually integrate the cabinets with the room's architecture. Simple one-piece crown molding is available in a variety of profiles to match the style of your kitchen cabinets, and is easily cut and installed. You can also make your own with a table-mounted router and a couple of bits *(see back endpaper)*. When choosing crown molding, make sure it is properly proportioned for the kitchen; molding that is too wide will have the effect of lowering the ceiling. Molding 3 or 4 inches in

Custom crown molding is available with elaborate carved patterns and scrollwork, in a wide range of modern and antique styles (left).

width is about right for an average 8-foot-high ceiling.

While cutting mitered corners at the end of a cabinet run requires care, the real challenge in installing crown molding is attaching it firmly and invisibly to the cabinets, particularly when there is only enough space between the cabinet tops and the ceiling for the molding itself. Attaching a nailer to the molding *(below)* allows it to be fastened to the cabinet from underneath.

Crown molding does not have to extend all the way to the ceiling. In the case of exceptionally high ceilings, there may be a gap of as much as a foot. This hidden space above the cabinet can be used to good effect; by placing fluorescent lights on top of the cabinets, the resulting indirect lighting can add sophistication to your kitchen.

INSTALLING CROWN MOLDING

1 Attaching the nailer
To provide an anchor for the fasteners when installing crown molding, attach a nailer to the molding first. Rip a ¾-by-1½-inch piece of stock equal in length to the piece of molding you are installing on the cabinet. To ease painting or finishing, the nailer should be cut from the same material as the molding. Protecting the stock with wood pads, glue the edge of the nailer flush to the bottom edge of the molding; support the two pieces with a shim as you clamp them together *(right)*. Repeat for the other pieces of molding.

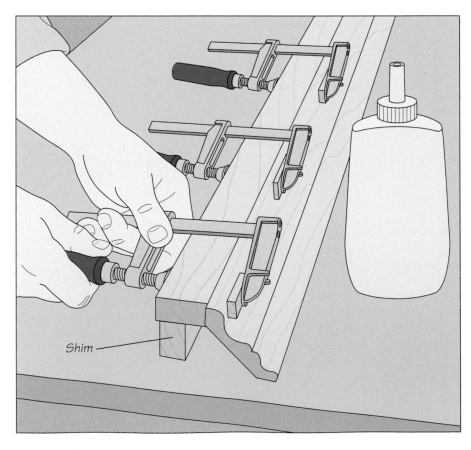

Shim

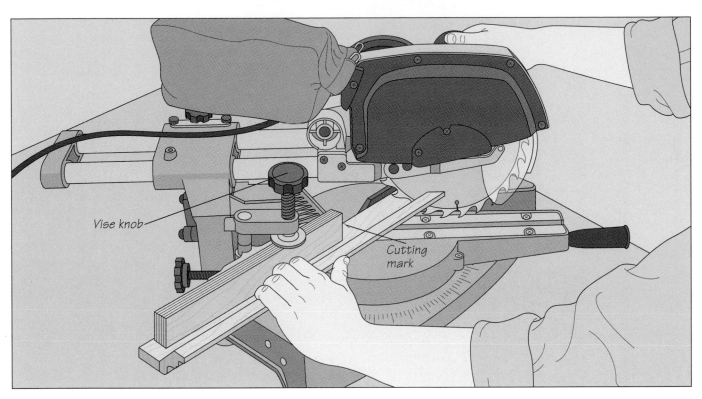

2 Cutting the molding to length

Mark the length of the top of the cabinet run on the upper face of the nailer. Set your miter saw to cut a 45° angle and position the molding right-side up on the saw so the mark is aligned with the blade. Secure the molding in place with the saw's vise knob; use a scrap piece of wood if necessary. Make the cut, keeping your hand well clear of the blade *(above)*.

3 Installing the molding

Position the crown molding on top of the cabinet run, aligning the heel of the miter you cut in step 2 with the corner of the cabinet. The nailer should extend out over the exterior of the cabinet front by the thickness of the doors. If there is sufficient space, screw the crown molding to the top of the cabinets through the nailers, spacing the fasteners every 6 to 8 inches. Otherwise, drive the fasteners from underneath. Miter the piece of crown molding for the end of the cabinet, then screw it in place *(left)*.

COUNTERTOPS

A tile backsplash can elevate an ordinary kitchen into a work of art. In the kitchen shown above, a backsplash of decorative ceramic tiles is carried over into an elaborate mural in the open space above the range, providing a traditional contrast to the clean, modern lines of the cabinets.

As indispensable to the kitchen as a workbench is to the shop, the countertop bears the brunt of the kitchen's workload. In addition to supporting the preparation and cooking of meals, the counter is also an all-purpose work surface used for scores of other daily household tasks, from brewing coffee to writing letters, from fixing appliances to sundry arts and crafts activities. It must be solid enough to stand on, easily cleaned with a damp cloth, and durable enough to look as good after 10 years as the day it was installed.

Fortunately, the technical innovations that transformed kitchen cabinetmaking in the post-war era have made this kind of performance commonplace. In particular, the perfection of plastic laminate has put attractive and resilient countertops within the reach of even the tightest of homebuilding budgets. Solid-surface materials sold under such brand names as Corian and Avonite offer even better performance—but at a price. And there still is a place in the kitchen for natural materials like wood and stone. The guide on page 122 will help you choose the best counter surface for your kitchen; the pages that follow outline the procedures and techniques necessary to install it.

While installation methods differ somewhat among countertop materials, there are many similarities. The procedure for installing a sink in a countertop with a plastic laminate surface *(page 125)*, for example, can be easily adapted to other countertops. One of the appeals of plastic laminate is its ease of application *(page 126)*. The original fitting need not be painstakingly exact; once the laminate is glued in place, it can be trimmed perfectly flush with the substrate using a laminate trimmer. This custom-fitting ability is particularly useful when melding the top sheet of laminate with a contrasting edge treatment *(page 137)*. Plastic laminate is the material used to make inexpensive, popular pre-molded counter tops *(page 132)*. These countertops have the top, edge treatment, and backsplash combined in one unit, and take much of the work out of installing a countertop. Solid-surface countertops *(page 129)* are more difficult to install but the results are rewarding. The ability to mold edges and execute invisible joints and repairs has made solid-surface countertops second only to plastic laminate in popularity, despite their higher cost.

Getting all the details right is the mark of true craftsmanship, and installing a backsplash *(pages 134-136)* is an excellent way to add an individual touch to your kitchen. Since a backsplash does not bear as much abuse as a countertop, you have considerably more leeway when choosing the material. Wood and tile, which can be problematic as countertop surfaces, are excellent choices for backsplashes. Selecting the perfect piece of hardwood or using ceramic tiles with an antique hand-painted pattern as a backsplash could be the difference that makes your kitchen unique.

Solid-surface countertop materials offer superior joint-cutting and shaping abilities. The kitchen at left features countertops made from Corian, a popular solid-surface material. Note the molded corners and seamless transition from countertop to sink.

A GALLERY OF COUNTERTOP SURFACES

The ideal countertop is not only attractive, durable, heat-resistant and waterproof, but easy to form, install, and repair, and inexpensive. Alas, this wonder has yet to be invented. Fortunately, there are several products, both man-made and natural, that come close.

Plastic laminate is the most common countertop facing material. First created in 1913, this material is formed by bonding paper, phenolic resins, and melamine plastic under heat and pressure. Plastic laminate has since become the standard, covering millions of tables and counters around the world.

Made of cast acrylic and polyester, solid-surface countertops were invented in the late 1960s, and are the closest to an ideal counter surface, but for their expense. If your budget permits, you can opt for the opulence of stone, such as granite or marble. Wood can be a very attractive counter, but many people shy away from using it near the sink where it will become wet.

Some of the best-designed kitchens make use of several contrasting materials, taking advantage of their different strengths. For example, a counter might be mostly wood or tile but switch to stainless steel around the sink. Another option is a plastic laminate or solid-surface countertop with an inset cutting board of wood. Lastly, do not forget the decorative possibilities of the backsplash, where the use of either wood or tiles can add a hand-crafted touch.

Plastic laminate is tough, inexpensive, and relatively easy to apply. Because it is paper thin, however, it cannot be shaped and is very difficult to repair.

Solid-surface material, such as Corian or Avonite, is expensive, but can be worked much like wood, since the pattern and color is consistent through its entire thickness. It can also be joined or repaired with invisible results.

Granite is the most prestigious—and expensive—material for countertops: extremely hard, smooth, and ideal for rolling pastry dough. It is also heavy and difficult to install.

Tile is heat- and water-resistant and available in a variety of patterns, colors, and finishes. The grout between the tiles can become stained and mildewed unless a high-quality epoxy grout is used.

Marble is very expensive but is not as tough as granite. And like granite, it needs to be cut and polished professionally.

Wooden countertops are warm and pleasant—well suited for country-style kitchens, but the least durable of the lot. They are best used for part of a counter, such as a chopping block insert.

INSTALLING COUNTERTOPS

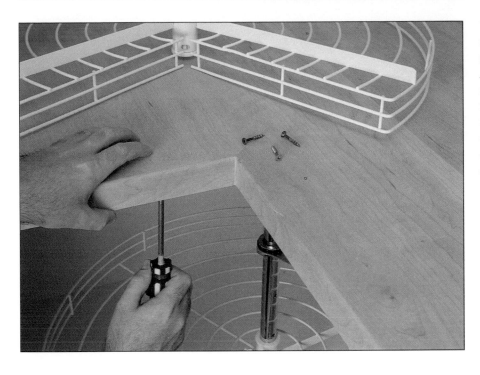

Wooden and plastic laminate countertops are installed by simply screwing them to the supporting cabinets. In the photo at left, a wooden countertop with mitered solid wood edging is being secured to a corner cabinet that features a lazy Susan; the fasteners are driven through the cabinet's countertop nailers into stretchers attached to the underside of the top.

BUILDING UP THE COUNTER

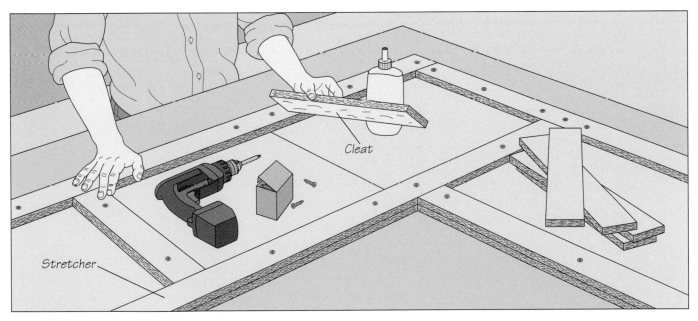

Cleat

Stretcher

Attaching stretching and cleats

Counter substrates are usually made of ¾-inch medium-density fiberboard, chosen for its dimensional stability. To double the perceived thickness of the countertop and increase its strength, build up the substrate with stretchers and cleats. First cut the substrate to size, making sure to include the amount of overhang; typically ¾ inch. Then prepare a number of 4-inch-wide stretchers and cleats of the same material as the substrate. Screw the stretchers along the edges of the substrate, then attach cleats between the stretchers, spacing them every 18 to 20 inches. If you are joining two sheets of substrate into an L-shaped countertop (above), make sure to secure a cleat on the joint.

CUTTING A HOLE FOR THE SINK

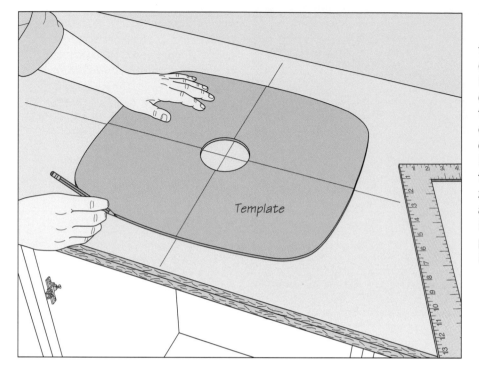

1 Marking the substrate

Most new sinks come with a template that will help you position and mark the opening on the substrate. If you do not have a template, you can make one from cardboard. Place the sink face down on the cardboard and trace its outline. Next draw a second line ½ inch inside the first one then cut out the template along this inner line. Draw a pair of lines dividing the template in half both vertically and horizontally. Center the sink on the substrate atop its lower cabinet, marking intersecting lines on the substrate. Place the template in position and align the two pairs of lines. Trace the outline with a pencil *(left)*.

2 Cutting the opening

Once you have marked out the position of the sink, check that the line does not cross any of the screws holding the stretchers and cleats. Next, drill a ½-inch access hole through the substrate just inside the perimeter. Install a combination blade in a saber saw and lower the blade through the hole. Holding the tool firmly, turn it on and start cutting along the line *(right)*. Try to cut as close to the line as possible. This need not be exact, as the edge will be hidden by the lip of the sink. To keep the waste piece from breaking off as you near the end of the cut, support it with your free hand. Solid-surface tops should never be cut with a saber saw; instead, use a router with a straight bit and a plywood template.

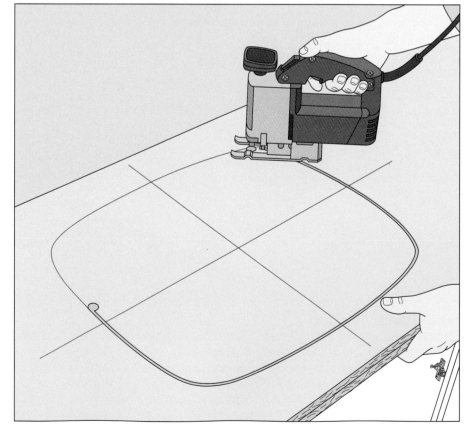

INSTALLING A LAMINATE COUNTERTOP

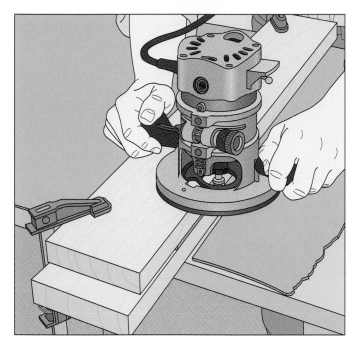

1 Trimming laminate

A sheet of plastic laminate can be ripped to width on your table saw, but it is easier to crosscut it with the jig shown here. To set up the jig, first joint two boards so they each have one straight edge. With a framing square, draw a line across the laminate at the desired length. Next, sandwich the laminate between the boards as shown. Align the line with the edges of the boards and clamp the whole assembly to the work surface. Install a flush-trimming bit in your router and set the cutting depth so the pilot bearing will rub against the jig. Place the router flat on the jig and ease the bit into the laminate, making sure the bearing rubs against the jig throughout the cut *(left)*. If a sheet is damaged at both ends, first trim one end to get a clean edge, then mark off the desired length and trim the other end. Cut the laminate at least an inch longer and wider than necessary; it can be trimmed flush later.

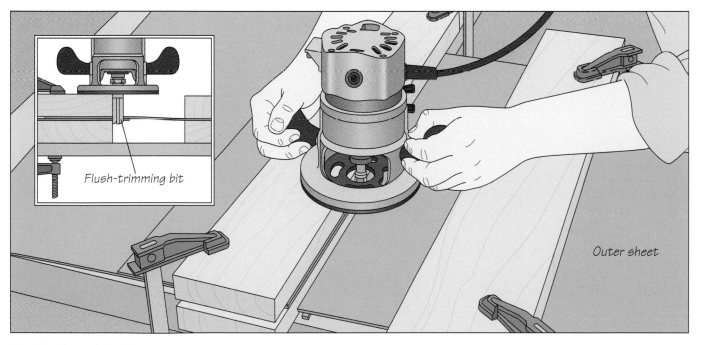

Flush-trimming bit

Outer sheet

2 Trimming matched pieces

Whenever two pieces of plastic laminate meet it is important that they match perfectly. Any gaps will be very noticeable and unattractive. Trimming the two sheets before installation in the jig shown here however will result in precisely matched edges every time. The procedure is similar to trimming a single sheet *(step 1)*. To set up the jig, secure both sheets between the boards, overlapping them by 4 to 5 inches, and clamp the assembly in place. To support the outer sheet, clamp it to the table in a second jig about 6 inches from the first *(inset)*. To trim the sheets, set the router on the jig with the pilot bearing against the edge, then pull it through the sheets *(above)*. Keep a slight pressure against the jig throughout the cut.

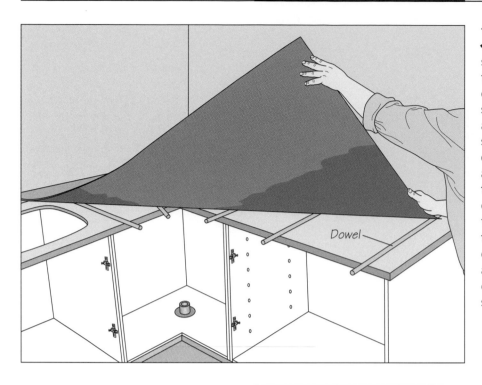

Dowel

3 Positioning the laminate

Attach the laminate sheet to the substrate with contact cement. First finish the edges of the substrate *(page 138)*; otherwise the edge of the laminate will show. Trim the sheet to approximate size, and joint any mating edges *(step 2)*. The sheet shown at left is for an L-shaped counter; the inside corner can be trimmed after gluing. Apply an even coat of contact cement to the substrate and let it dry. Then apply a thin coat to both surfaces and let dry until it is tacky. As contact cement bonds instantly, set ½-inch dowels on the substrate about 12 inches apart. Lay the laminate sheet on the dowels without letting it touch the substrate *(left)*.

4 Gluing down the laminate

Slide the laminate sheet over the dowels to position it properly; since the sheet is slightly oversized, you have some margin for error. Starting at one end, remove the first dowel and press the laminate against the substrate. Work toward the other end, removing dowels and pressing the laminate down as you go *(right)*. Press the laminate sheet against the substrate with a roller *(inset)*. If you are dealing with two matching sheets, draw a line across the substrate where the two sheets are to meet. When installing the first sheet, begin by laying down the edge starting at this line. To install the second sheet, begin by carefully butting its edge against the first piece.

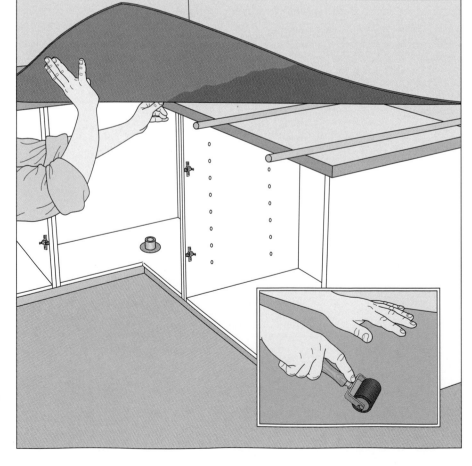

5 Trimming the edges

Use a router or laminate trimmer mounted with a flush-trimming bit to trim the edges of the laminate. First, remove any glue squeeze-out from the joint. Then set the cutting depth so the bearing will rub the middle of the substrate. To trim the edges, hold the trimmer flat on the counter and ease it into the laminate. Continue moving the trimmer along the edge *(right)*, working against the direction of bit rotation and keeping slight pressure against the substrate.

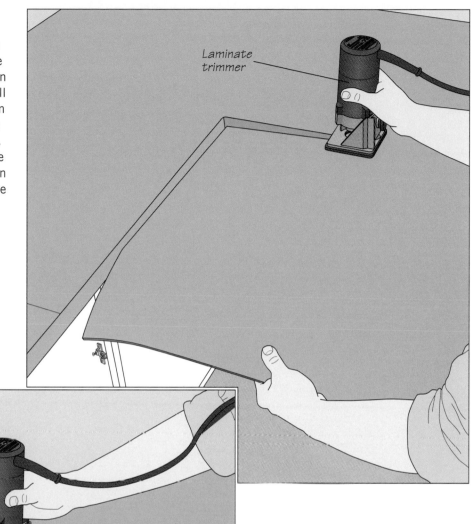

Laminate trimmer

6 Cutting out the sink opening

The laminate covering the sink opening can be cut out using the same method you used to trim the edges. Starting the cut, however, is a bit more tricky. You can either drill a hole through the laminate and use a regular bottom-mounted flush-trimming bit or you can equip a plunge router with a special panel pilot bit. This bit has a pointed tip that can penetrate the laminate; the shaft of the bit then acts as a pilot to guide the trimmer. Since this bit does not have a pilot bearing it may burn the edge, but this will be hidden under the sink.

7 Screwing the counter to the cabinet
Position the counter on the cabinet and anchor the counter with wood screws, driving them in from below *(right)*. Secure each screw through the cabinet's countertop nailers and into the stretchers attached to the underside of the countertop. Select the size of your fasteners carefully; too long a screw could pierce the laminate.

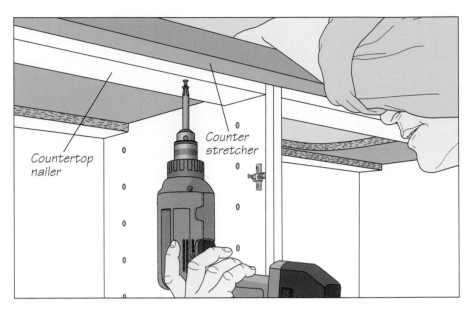

INSTALLING THE SINK

1 Testing the fit
Insert the sink into the counter to check the fit *(above)*. Trim the counter opening if necessary. Mark the holes on the countertop for the taps and cut them out with a hole saw. Apply plumber's putty to the underside of the sink rim. (Some sinks come with a special closed-cell foam tape that serves the same purpose.) Lower the sink into place *(above)* and adjust it so it rests square to the edge of the counter.

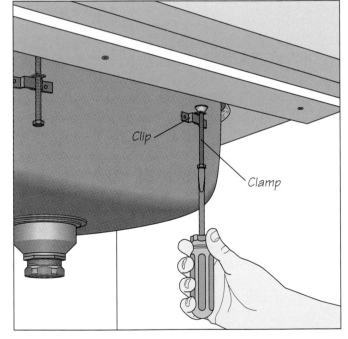

2 Securing the counter
The sink is held in place with special clamps that pull it down against the counter top. To install each clamp, insert its hook into the matching clip on the sink. Tighten it *(above)* until the serrated end touches the substrate. Once all the clamps are in place, begin to secure the sink as evenly as possible, gradually tightening each clamp a little at a time until the rim is flush with the countertop; avoid overtightening.

INSTALLING A SOLID-SURFACE COUNTERTOP

1 Attaching furring strips

Unlike particleboard, solid surface material expands and contracts with changes in temperature, so it cannot be attached to a full substrate. Instead, attach it directly to the cabinets or to furring strips. Furring strips add height to the countertop and allow a built-up edge to be added later. Cut a number of ¾-by-4-inch boards to match the depth of the countertop. Attach the strips to cabinet modules with wood screws, spacing them about 18 inches apart. Add an extra furring strip wherever two sheets are to be joined and 3 inches from either side of an opening for a sink or cooktop.

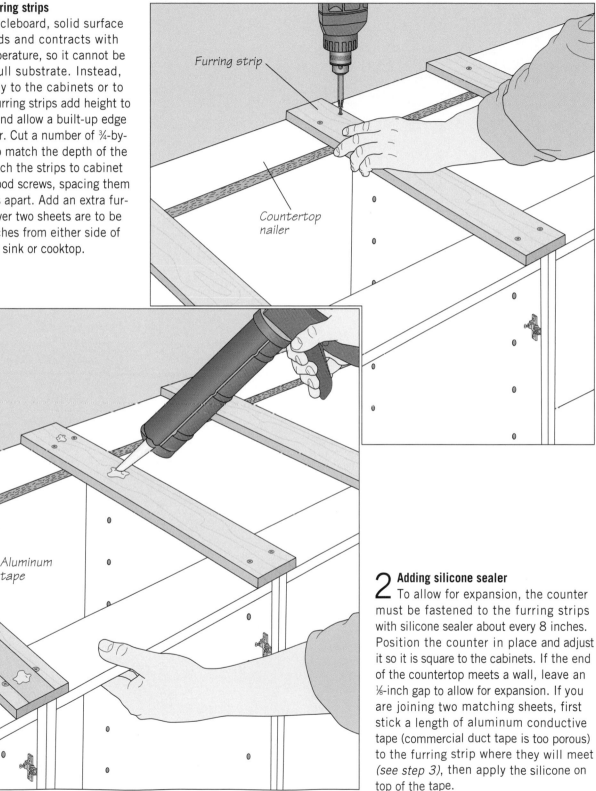

Furring strip

Countertop nailer

Aluminum tape

2 Adding silicone sealer

To allow for expansion, the counter must be fastened to the furring strips with silicone sealer about every 8 inches. Position the counter in place and adjust it so it is square to the cabinets. If the end of the countertop meets a wall, leave an ⅛-inch gap to allow for expansion. If you are joining two matching sheets, first stick a length of aluminum conductive tape (commercial duct tape is too porous) to the furring strip where they will meet (see step 3), then apply the silicone on top of the tape.

3 Joining the sheets
Lay the first sheet of solid-surface material in place on the furring strips, clamping it to keep it from moving. Lay the second sheet in place, arranging it so there is an even gap of $\frac{1}{16}$ inch between the two sheets. Work quickly; the silicone will set within 20 minutes, making the countertop difficult to move. Make a dam under the gap where it overhangs the cabinets with some aluminum conductive tape *(left)*.

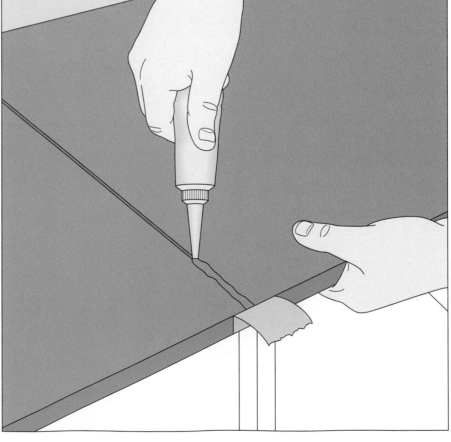

4 Applying joint adhesive
Selecting the right color and pattern to match the countertop, prepare a tube of solid-surface joint adhesive according to manufacturer's directions. (This usually involves injecting a tube of catalyst into a larger tube of adhesive and mixing the two.) Fill the gap half full with the mixture, working from back to front. Be sure to keep the tube vertical. Push the sheets together to squeeze out the excess adhesive. Pop any air bubbles with a toothpick and add extra adhesive to areas where the adhesive lies below the surface of the countertop. Do not remove the excess; it will be sanded down later.

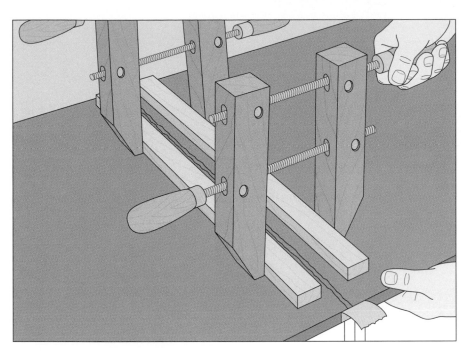

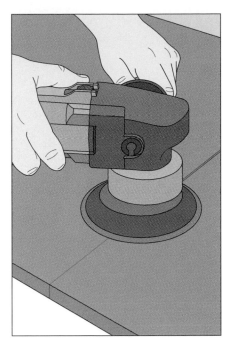

5 Clamping the sheets together

Attach a strip of wood to the countertop on either side of the gap with beads of hot-melt glue. Clamp a pair of handscrews to the strips to pull the two sheets snugly together. Do not clamp them too tightly since this can squeeze out all the adhesive. Let the glue cure for one hour, then loosen the clamps and tap off the wood strips. Use a putty knife with rounded edges to remove any leftover hot glue.

6 Smoothing the surface

Remove the excess adhesive and level the joint with a block plane. Make sure the blade is very sharp and the corners are slightly rounded. A belt sander with 120-grit paper will also work but it produces much more dust and runs the risk of gouging the counter. Smooth the joint further with a random orbit sander using 180-grit sandpaper *(above)*. To keep the dust down, moisten the counter. Finally, buff the entire surface with a synthetic polishing pad. Again, keep the surface moist. The final joint should be perfectly invisible.

Since their color and pattern run through their entire thickness, solid-surface countertops offer unmatched shaping and joinery abilities. In the photo at left, a solid-surface countertop is bonded seamlessly with a sink of the same material. The built-in drain board to the right of the sink was made by routing grooves in the countertop with a carbide-tipped bit.

INSTALLING A PRE-MOLDED COUNTERTOP

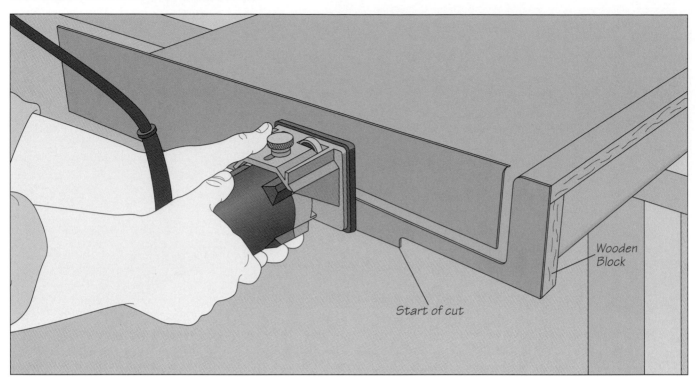

Wooden Block

Start of cut

1 Laminating the countertop end

Apply plastic laminate to the visible end of a pre-molded counter to hide any gaps or exposed edges. For example, when the counter is pushed against the wall there will be a wide gap on the exposed end between the backsplash and the wall. Fill this gap with a wooden block. To cover the end, use a pre-formed strip or cut a rectangle of laminate slightly oversize, then affix it to the counter with contact cement. Install a bottom-mounted flush-trimming bit in a router or laminate trimmer and set the cutting depth to about ½ inch. To trim the end, ease the bit into the laminate, then move the bit all around its edges *(above)*. Keep the base of the tool flat against the end to ensure a smooth cut.

2 Joining pre-molded countertops

Pre-molded countertops are typically available in lengths up to 12 feet long, so they rarely have to be joined in a cabinet run. Corner joints, however, are common. Cutting a pre-molded countertop at a perfect 45° angle is tricky, though, and is a job best left to a professional with a large radial-arm saw. Joining the countertops with counter connectors afterward is somewhat easier. Place the two sections face-down on a work surface and butt the mating edges of the joint together. To place the connectors, make a mark across the joint 6 inches from either end. Referring to the marks, drill a 35mm-diameter recess on either side of the joint, set back 1½ inches from the joint. Form a channel between the recesses for the bolt by making two cuts with a dovetail saw, then cleaning out the waste with a chisel. To join the two countertops, align them, insert the connectors, and tighten them with a wrench until they are both snug *(right)*. Check that the countertops are perfectly aligned and flush, then finish tightening the connectors.

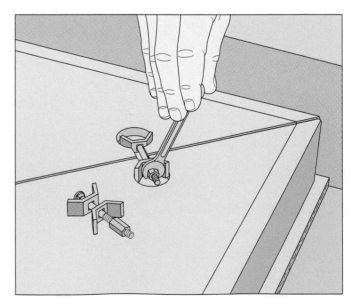

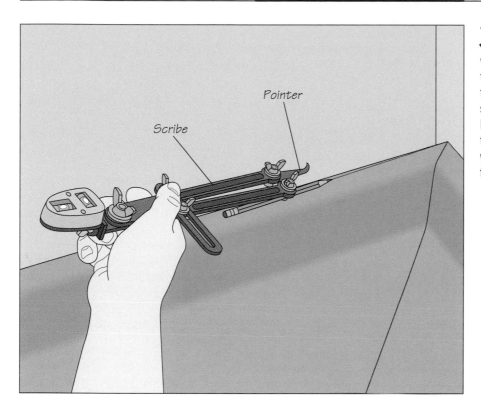

Pointer

Scribe

3 Scribing the backsplash
Since walls are seldom straight, you will probably need to scribe to fit the wall, then sand down the high spots. Position the countertop in place and set a transfer scribe slightly wider than the distance between the wall and the lip. Hold the tool as shown at left then pull it along the wall to mark the backsplash. Repeat for the other wall.

4 Sanding backsplash
As the lip of the backsplash is only about ¾ inch thick, it is fairly easy to sand into shape. With a very light touch sand down to the scribed line with a belt sander *(below)*. Hold the sander against the edge at an angle so it will remove slightly more material from the bottom edge than the top. This will ensure a very close fit at the wall. Repeat for the other wall.

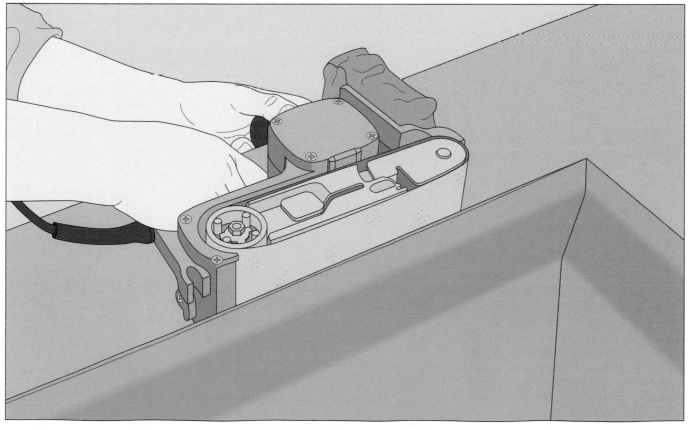

BACKSPLASHES AND EDGE TREATMENTS

MAKING A TILE BACKSPLASH

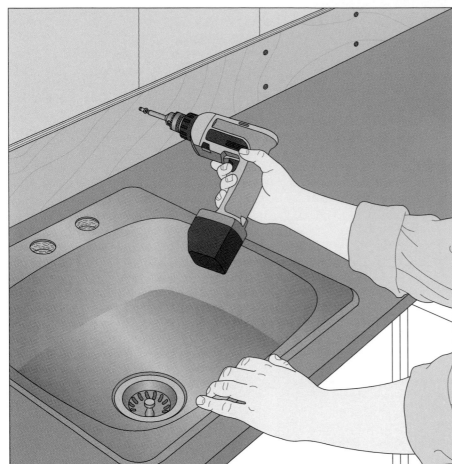

1 Attaching the substrate
To provide a gluing surface and to add depth to a tile backsplash, screw a ½-inch-thick plywood substrate to the wall first. Determining the correct length of the substrate can be tricky because tiles are of fixed width and the end of the backsplash usually will not fall at the counter's end. The end of the backsplash is usually slightly set back *(see page 136)*. To find the correct length, lay out all the tiles on the counter with an ⅛ inch space between them and cut the substrate to this length; rip it equal to the height of the tiles plus ⅛ inch. Mark the placement of the studs on the wall, then secure the plywood with two screws in each stud *(left)*. If necessary, use two pieces of plywood trimmed so they join at a stud.

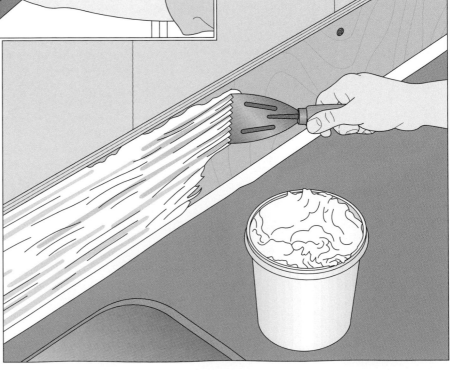

2 Applying mastic
Clean the plywood with a slightly dampened cloth to pick up any dust. Protect the countertop with masking tape, and apply a generous coat of mastic with a serrated trowel, smoothing it as you go to create a surface like a freshly plowed field. Do not try to cover too large an area at first; the mastic sets in about 30 minutes.

3 Mounting the tiles

Cut ⅛-inch-thick spacers to separate the tiles. Make sure the tiles are all clean and dust free. Starting in one corner, place two spacers on the counter in front of the wall where the first tile will go. Set the tile on the spacers and pivot it into place, separating it from the wall corner with another spacer. Press the tile against the substrate, giving it a slight twist to ensure a tight fit. Then install the rest of the tiles, separating them with spacers *(right)*.

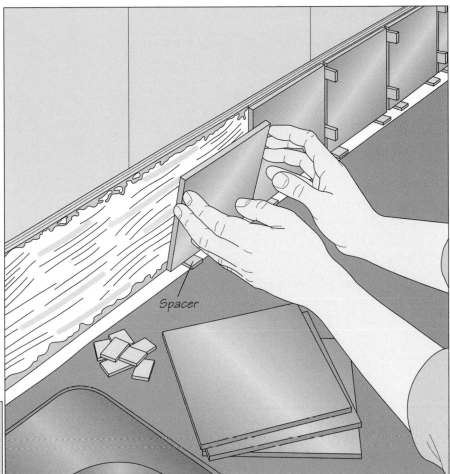

Spacer

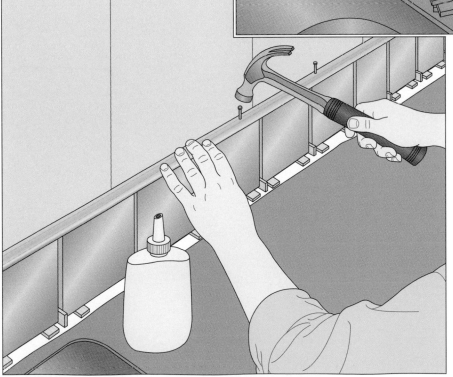

4 Attaching molding

Add molding to the top of the backsplash after the tile mastic has cured. The width of the molding should be equal to the combined thickness of the substrate and the tiles. Miter the end of the molding, then trim it to length. Apply a bead of glue to the plywood substrate then place the molding in position. Fasten it to the substrate with a finishing nail every 5 to 6 inches. Remove the masking tape and seal the tiles by filling all the gaps with epoxy grout, and applying a joint of silicone between the tiles and countertop.

INSTALLING A WOODEN BACKSPLASH

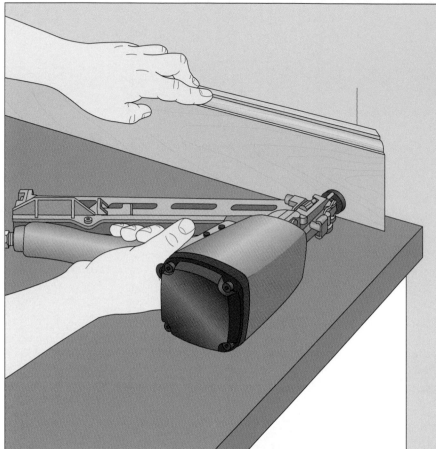

1 Attaching the backsplash
To make a wooden backsplash with molded top and side edges, install a square-edged board, then add a molding *(page 135)* or shape the edge of a wider board with a router or shaper and install the backsplash in one piece. In either case, select a length of attractive hardwood for your backsplash and plane it to a thickness of ¾ to ⅞ inch. Cut it to size, making it slightly shorter than the countertop to create a setback at the end. Miter the ends as shown. Indicate the placement of each stud with a light mark on the wall, then nail the board in place *(left)*.

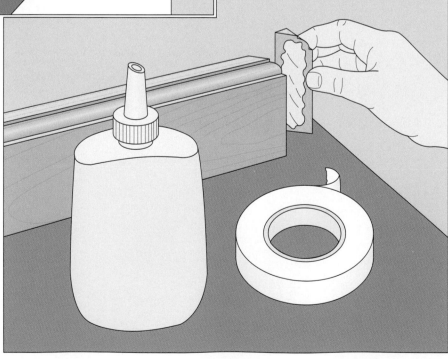

2 Installing a return
Where the backsplash ends, make a return molding from some scrap leftover from the backsplash. Miter the return so it fills the gap between the backsplash and the wall, forming a square end and continuing the molded profile. Since this piece will not be subjected to a lot of stress it can be simply glued in place and then held with some masking tape until the glue cures.

A chamfering bit reveals a walnut divider between plastic laminate top and edge surfaces. This effect was created by applying a solid wood edge to the counter substrate, then adding laminate to the top and edge. Not only is this an attractive way to ease the counter front but it also disguises the dark edges of the laminate.

INSTALLING A DECORATIVE EDGING

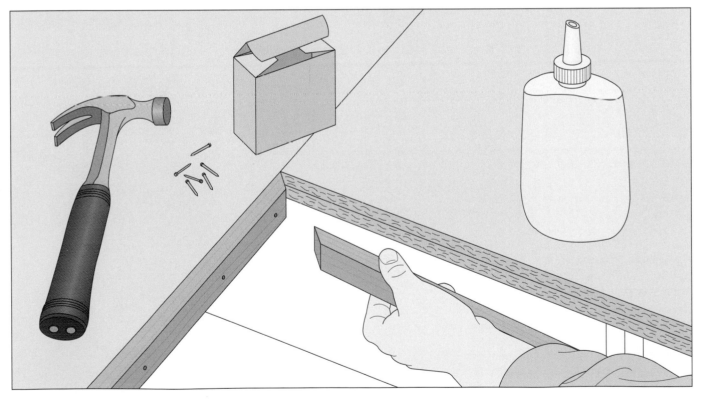

1 Applying wooden edging

Apply solid wood edging to the countertop before you glue down the plastic laminate top *(page 126)*. (This will ensure there are no cracks between the upper laminate and the edging.) Mill the edge stock to a thickness of ½ inch and the desired width.

Spread a film of glue on the wood, then fasten the piece in place with finishing nails every 4 to 6 inches. If the edge will be chamfered *(step 3)*, place the nails at least ½ inch below the top edge; this will protect the router bit from being damaged.

2 Applying laminate

Trim a length of plastic laminate a bit wider than the thickness of the counter. Fasten it to the counter edge with contact cement *(left)* and press it down firmly with a roller. When the adhesive has cured, trim the laminate flush with a router or laminate trimmer. Use a chisel to square up any inside corners, then remove any excess contact cement with a scraper. Once this is done, apply laminate to the countertop *(pages 125-127)*.

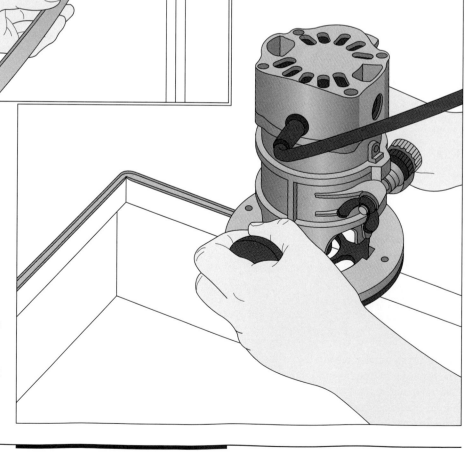

3 Chamfering the edge

By chamfering the corners of the built-up edging, you will expose the wood edge you added in the first step. Install a piloted chamfering bit in your router and set the cutting depth to ⅜ inch. Holding the tool with its base flat on the countertop, ease the bit into the laminate until the bearing touches the counter edge. Move the tool around the counter, working it against the direction of bit rotation. The bit cannot cut right into the apex of an inside corner, but the resulting lamb's tongue pattern is an attractive effect.

MOLDING A WOODEN EDGE

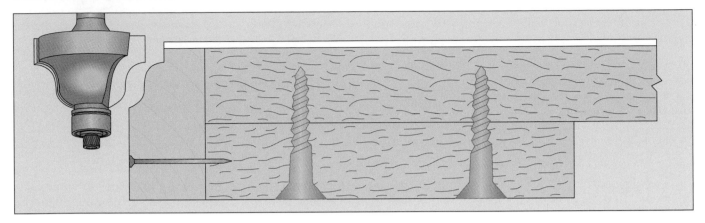

Routing an ogee profile

Nail a solid wood strip to the edge of the counter *(page 137)* before gluing the plastic laminate down on the countertop. Since you will be shaping the edge with a router, make sure to place the fasteners well below the bit's depth of cut *(above)*. Next, attach the laminate top and trim it flush *(pages 126-127)*. To shape the edge, install a piloted ogee or other edge-forming bit in your router. Set the tool on the counter and adjust the cutting depth so the bearing will ride against the lower edge of the counter. To shape the edge, set the router flat on the countertop, then ease the bit into the wood. Move the router around the counter, working against the bit's direction of rotation.

ROUTING A DRIP EDGE IN A SOLID-SURFACE COUNTER

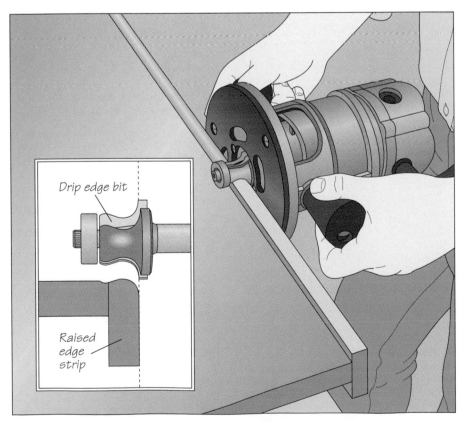

Drip edge bit

Raised edge strip

Shaping a drip edge

A drip edge is a slightly raised edge that prevents minor spills from running off the countertop. Apply a strip of matching solid-surface material to the edge of the countertop, creating a raised edge. Affix the edging with adhesive designed especially for the material *(pages 130-131)*. Install a piloted drip edge bit in your router and adjust the cutting depth so the top of the curve is even with the router base; the inset shows how the bit should meet the counter. To shape the counter, hold the router base against the edge, then lower it until the pilot bearing touches the countertop surface. Keeping the router pressed flat against the edge, move the tool along the counter *(left)*.

GLOSSARY

A-B-C-D

Adjustable leveller: Any commercial foot or leg attached to lower kitchen cabinets to level and support them.

Auxiliary fence: A wooden attachment to a tool's rip fence that serves to attach accessories and prevent accidental damage to the fence.

Backsplash: A continuation of the countertop along the back wall; can be part of the countertop itself or made from tile or wood.

Biscuit: A thin oval wafer of compressed wood that fits into a semicircular slot cut by a plate joiner.

Blank: A piece of solid or glued-up wood used to create a furniture part.

Board-and-batten door: A door made of boards fastened together with lap joints and held together by a diagonal batten.

Board foot: A unit of wood volume measurement equivalent to a piece of wood one inch thick, 12 inches long, and 12 inches wide.

Caul: In veneering or gluing up a carcase, a board placed between the clamps and the workpiece to distribute clamping pressure.

Chalk line: A length of twine loaded with chalk dust used to mark long lines that are normally either level or plumb.

Chamfer: A decorative bevel cut along the edge of a workpiece.

Cheek: The face of the projecting tenon in a mortise-and-tenon joint.

Cockbeading: A narrow decorative molding applied to the inside edges of a face frame or drawer opening.

Cope-and-stick joint: A method of joining stiles and rails in frame-and-panel construction. Tongues in the rails mesh with grooves in the stiles; a decorative molding is cut along the inside edge of the frame.

Counterbore: To drill a hole that permits the head of a screw to sit below the wood surface and be concealed with a wood plug.

Countersink: To drill a hole that permits the head of a screw to lie flush with or slightly below a wood surface.

Dado: A rectangular channel cut in a workpiece.

Dado head: A combination of blades and cutters used to form dadoes and grooves in wood. The assembly is mounted on a table saw with two blades separated by one to five cutters to achieve the right width.

Drip edge: A raised profile at the edge of a countertop that prevents spills.

E-F-G-H-I-J

Edge banding: Strips of material used to cover the edges of plywood and composite boards; can be solid wood or plastic laminate.

End grain: The arrangement and direction of the wood fibers running across the the ends of a board.

Face frame: A decorative wooden frame fixed around the front of a cabinet, providing extra rigidity to the cabinet.

False front: A piece of wood installed over a drawer front, usually to conceal the end grain of the sides or to create a lipped front.

Featherboard: A piece of wood with thin fingers or "feathers" along one end to hold a workpiece securely against the fence or table of a power tool.

Fence: An adjustable guide used to keep the edge of a workpiece a set distance from the cutting edge of a tool.

Filler strip: A thin strip of either wood or laminate-covered material used to conceal gaps between cabinets.

Furring strip: A narrow length of wood installed atop a lower cabinet to support the counter and raise its height.

Glass-stop molding: Decorative strips of wood used to hold panes of glass in a cabinet door.

Glazing bars: Molded strips of wood joined by half-laps to hold several panes of glass in a single cabinet door.

Inset drawer: A drawer that fits flush within a frameless cabinet.

Island: A freestanding cabinet or cabinet run isolated from the walls of a kitchen.

Jig: A device for guiding a tool or holding workpiece in position.

K-L-M-N-O-P-Q

Kickback: The tendency of a workpiece to be thrown back in the direction of the operator of a woodworking machine.

Kickplate: The board that covers the toe kick of a lower kitchen cabinet or the exposed faces of a plinth.

Laminate trimmer: A lightweight router used to trim plastic laminate and solid wood edging flush with its substrate.

Lock miter joint: A joint cut with a special router bit that produces an interlocking connection with a mitered outside corner.

Melamine: A popular brand of plastic laminate made from bonded plastic, paper, and phenolic resin; available in sheets or bonded to plywood or particleboard.

Miter gauge: A device that slides in a slot on a saw or router table, providing support for the stock as it moves past the blade or bit; can be adjusted to different angles for miter cuts.

Mortise-and-tenon joint: A joinery technique in which a projecting tenon cut in one board fits into a matching hole, or mortise, in another.

Mortise: A hole cut into a piece of wood to receive a tenon.

Nailer rails: Wooden rails attached to the backs of cabinets that support the cabinets when screwed to the wall studs.

Overlay drawer: A drawer that partially or fully overlays the frame of a face frame cabinet.

Panel saw: A track-mounted circular saw used for accurate cuts of large sheet goods such as plywood.

Plainsawn veneer: Veneer that has been cut from the log in a flat sheet; hardwood plywood with plainsawn face veneer closely resembles solid wood.

Plinth: A mitered wooden frame that acts as a base for lower cabinets or islands.

Push block or stick: A device used to feed a workpiece into a blade or cutter to protect the operator's fingers.

R-S

Rabbet: A step-like cut in the edge or end of a board; usually forms part of a joint.

Rail: The horizontal member of a frame-and-panel assembly. See *stile*.

Ready-to-assemble (RTA) fastener: A type of threaded fastener with a stout shaft and a narrow head; used for fast assembly of cabinets.

Scribing: Marking a line with a compass or scribing tool to copy the irregularity of a wall onto a cabinet or counter where it butts against a wall. Once the wood is planed or sanded to this line, the cabinet or counter will fit seamlessly against the wall.

Shim: A thin, wedge-shaped piece of material used to level cabinets and fill minor irregularities.

Shoulder: In a mortise-and-tenon joint, the part of the tenon that is perpendicular to the cheek.

Solid-surface material: A composite board made of cast acrylic and polyester used for kitchen countertops; sold under such names as Corian and Avonite.

Stile: The vertical member of a frame-and-panel assembly. See *rail*.

Story pole: A long, thin piece of wood with the measurements for a project indicated on its length.

Stud finder: A device that electronically pinpoints the location of wall studs.

T-U-V-W-X-Y-Z

Tambour door: A type of door made from narrow slats attached to a flexible canvas backing that slides in tracks routed in the sides of the carcase.

Tearout: The tendency of a blade or cutter to tear wood fibers.

Template: A pattern used to guide a tool in reproducing identical copies of a piece.

Tenon: A protrusion from the end of a workpiece that fits into a mortise.

Three-wing slotting cutter: A piloted, groove-cutting router bit.

Toe kick: The recess running along the bottom of a lower cabinet that allows space for the feet of a person standing before the cabinet.

Tongue-and-groove joint: A joint in which a tongue cut in the edge or end of one piece fits into a groove in the mating piece.

Transfer scribe: A compass-like device that transfers the profile of one surface onto another.

Utility hookup: The point where utilities such as water, sewage, and electricity are connected.

Wood movement: The shrinking or swelling of wood in reaction to changes in relative humidity.

Work triangle: An ergonomic principle measuring the efficiency of a workspace that connects the three most common places of work in that space; in a kitchen, typically the refrigerator, stove, and sink.

INDEX

ACKNOWLEDGMENTS

The editors wish to thank the following:

LAYOUT AND DESIGN
Lee Valley Tools, Ltd., Ottawa, Ont.; Stanley Tools, Division of the Stanley Works,
New Britain, CT; Tritech Industries, St-Lambert, Que.

CASEWORK
Adjustable Clamp Co., Chicago, IL; American Clamping (Canada) Inc., Cambridge, Ont.;
Black & Decker/Elu Power Tools, Towson, MD; Bradbury Industries, Toronto, Ont.;
Canadian Industrial Distributors, Inc., Montreal, Que.; CMT Tools, Oldsmar, FL;
Delta International Machinery/Porter-Cable, Guelph, Ont.; Freud Westmore Tools, Ltd.,
Mississauga, Ont.; Hitachi Power Tools U.S.A. Ltd., Norcross, GA;
Julius Blum Inc., Stanley, NC; Lee Valley Tools, Ltd., Ottawa, Ont.; Modulus, St-Hubert, Que.;
Les Realisations Loeven-Morcel, Montreal, Que.; Sears, Roebuck and Co., Chicago, IL;
Senco Products, Inc., Cincinnati, OH; Steiner-Lamello A.G.
Switzerland/Colonial Saw Co., Kingston, MA; Tool Trend Ltd., Concord, Ont.

DOORS
Adjustable Clamp Co., Chicago, IL; American Tool Cos., Lincoln, NE; CMT Tools, Oldsmar, FL;
Delta International Machinery/Porter-Cable, Guelph, Ont.; Great Neck Saw Mfrs. Inc. (Buck Bros.
Division), Millbury, MA; Julius Blum Inc., Stanley, NC; Sears, Roebuck and Co., Chicago, IL;
Steiner-Lamello A.G. Switzerland/Colonial Saw Co., Kingston, MA; Tool Trend Ltd., Concord, Ont.

DRAWERS
Adjustable Clamp Co., Chicago, IL; Delta International Machinery/Porter-Cable, Guelph, Ont.;
David Keller, Petaluma, CA; Julius Blum Inc., Stanley, NC; Sears, Roebuck and Co., Chicago, IL;
Stanley Tools, Division of the Stanley Works, New Britain, CT; Steiner-Lamello A.G.
Switzerland/Colonial Saw Co., Kingston, MA; Tool Trend Ltd., Concord, Ont.

INSTALLING CABINETS
Adjustable Clamp Co., Chicago, IL; Delta International Machinery/Porter-Cable, Guelph, Ont.;
Hitachi Power Tools U.S.A. Ltd., Norcross, GA; Julius Blum Inc., Stanley, NC;
Lee Valley Tools, Ltd., Ottawa, Ont.; Ornamental Mouldings, High Point, NC; Sears,
Roebuck and Co., Chicago, IL; Stanley Tools, Division of the Stanley Works, New Britain, CT;
Steiner-Lamello A.G. Switzerland/Colonial Saw Co., Kingston, MA; Tritech Industries, St-Lambert, Que.

COUNTERTOPS
Adjustable Clamp Co., Chicago, IL; Avonite, Inc., Sylmar, CA; Black & Decker/Elu Power Tools,
Towson, MD; CMT Tools, Oldsmar, FL; Delta International Machinery/Porter-Cable, Guelph, Ont.;
Lee Valley Tools, Ltd., Ottawa, Ont.; Sears, Roebuck and Co., Chicago, IL;
Senco Products, Inc., Cincinnati, OH

The following persons also assisted in the preparation of this book:

Lorraine Doré, Kerry & Victoria McCluggage, Scott Yetman

PICTURE CREDITS

Cover Robert Chartier
6,7 Carolyn Jones
8,9 Gary Moss
10,11 Michael Tincher
14,15,27,38,79 Brian Vanden Brink
87 Courtesy Julius Blum, Inc.
112 Brian Vanden Brink
118 Courtesy Ornamental Mouldings
120,121 Brian Vanden Brink
131 Courtesy Avonite, Inc.